Blow the Trumpet in Zion!

Blow the Trumpet in Zion!

Global Vision and Action for the 21st-century Black Church

Edited by Iva E. Carruthers, Frederick D. Haynes III, and Jeremiah A. Wright Jr.

Fortress Press
Minneapolis

Video cassettes of keynote addresses from the Samuel DeWitt Proctor Conference are available at www.tucc.org or e-mail info@sdpconference.info

Cover design: Brad Norr Design
Interior design: Becky Lowe
Editor: Katara Washington

Library of Congress Cataloging-in-Publication Data
Blow the trumpet in Zion! Global vision and action for the twenty-first-century Black church / edited by Iva E. Carruthers, Frederick D. Haynes III, and Jeremiah A. Wright Jr.
   p. cm.
Includes bibliographical references.
ISBN 0-8006-3712-7 (alk. paper)
   1. African Americans—Religion—Congresses. 2. African American churches—Congresses. 3. Christianity and justice—Congresses. I. Carruthers, Iva E., 1945– II. Haynes, Frederick D., 1960– III. Wright, Jeremiah A., Jr.
BR563.N4B58 2005
277.3'083'08996073—dc22
                                        2004024212

The paper used in this publication meets the minimum requirements of American National Standard for Information Sciences—Permanence of Paper for Printed Library Materials, ANSI Z329.48-1984.

Manufactured in the U.S.A.
09 08 07 06 05 1 2 3 4 5 6 7 8 9 10

to
Samuel DeWitt Proctor

Ella P. Mitchell
Henry H. Mitchell
Gardner C. Taylor
Wyatt Tee Walker

Contents

Contributors

CHARLES G. ADAMS is Senior Pastor of Hartford Memorial Baptist Church in Detroit. An internationally acclaimed preacher and theologian, he teaches at the Ecumenical Theological Seminary in Detroit. He serves on the board of trustees of Morehouse College and the visiting Committee of Harvard Divinity School. He is the author of many publications, including *Power in the Pulpit*.

RANDALL C. BAILEY is the Andrew W. Mellon Professor of Hebrew Scripture at the Interdenominational Theological Center in Atlanta. He has studied and lectured throughout the world and concentrates on the relationship of Ancient Africa and the Hebrew Bible. He is the author of many publications, including *David in Love and War: The Pursuit of Power in 2 Samuel 10-12* and *Yet with a Steady Beat: Contemporary U.S. Afrocentric Biblical Interpretation*.

IVA E. CARRUTHERS is General Secretary of the Samuel DeWitt Proctor Conference and Founder/Director of Lois House, an urban ministry and retreat renewal center. She is Professor Emeritus of Sociology at Northeastern Illinois University and has published numerous articles. Her work, *The Church and Reparations*, was translated into four languages and presented at the 2001 UN Conference on Racism. She has produced award-winning software and educational television and video programs.

DELMAN L. COATES is the Senior Pastor of Mount Ennon Baptist Church in Clinton, Maryland. He is completing doctoral work in New Testament studies and Early Christian history, examining the implications for the Black Church in the 21st century. He has served as a grants officer in the Corporate Social Responsibility Division of J.P. Morgan Chase & Company in New York.

JAMES H. CONE is the Charles A. Briggs Distinguished Professor of Systematic Theology at Union Theological Seminary in New York. Author of eleven books and over 150 articles, his first book,

Black Theology and Black Power, is considered a seminal work in Black Liberation theology and religious scholarship in the United States. He is a founding member of the Society for the Study of Black Religion and the Ecumenical Association of Third World Theologians.

STACEY L. EDWARDS is Associate Pastor/Singles Minister at Trinity United Church of Christ in Chicago. Her innovation in ministry and pastoral care for singles has become a national model and includes a Friday noon worship service for persons working in downtown Chicago.

JAMES A. FORBES JR. is Senior Pastor of Riverside Church in New York City and is the first African American to serve the largest multi-cultural congregation in the nation. He has been at the forefront of national leadership in fostering and organizing interfaith and ecumenical dialogues. In their March 4, 1996 issue, *Newsweek* magazine recognized Forbes as one of the 12 "most effective preachers" in the English-speaking world.

JACQUELYN GRANT is the Fuller E. Callaway Professor of Systematic Theology at the Interdenominational Theological Center. Her groundbreaking work in theology was pivotal to the development of Womanist theology. She is the author of the best-selling book, *White Women's Christ and Black Women's Jesus.*

FREDERICK D. HAYNES, III is Senior Pastor of Friendship-West Baptist Church in Dallas. Under his leadership Friendship-West is developing a 60-acre multi-purpose Christian community. Through his preaching and media ministry he has reached millions throughout the world. He is completing a doctorate in Ministry at Oxford University and is recognized as one of the most dynamic religious leaders of his generation.

OBERY M. HENDRICKS JR. is Professor of Biblical Interpretation at New York Theological Seminary. He is the recipient of many academic awards and is a member of the Advisory Translation Committee of the New Revised Standard Version Bible and commentator on the Gospel of John in the Oxford Annotated New Revised Standard Bible. In addition to publishing many scholarly articles, he is also the author of an award-winning novel, *Living Water.*

Asa G. Hilliard, III is the Fuller E. Callaway Professor of Urban Education at Georgia State University. He has authored more than 300 publications. His most recent books are *The Maroon within Us: Selected Essays on African American Community Socialization* and *SBA: The Reawakening of the African Mind.*

Dwight N. Hopkins is Professor of Theology at the University of Chicago. He has authored or edited many publications, including fourteen books. His books include *Shoes That Fit Our Feet; Introducing Black Theology of Liberation; Down, Up and Over: Slave Religion and Black Theology;* and *Black Faith and Public Talk.* His newest work is *On Being Human: Black Theology Looks at Culture, Self and Race.*

Monifa A. Jumanne is noted for her faith-based work on HIV-AIDS and author of "Affirming a Future with Hope: HIV and Substance Abuse Prevention for African American Communities of Faith." She is the former Executive Director of the Health Education and Leadership Project at Interdenominational Theological Center.

Samuel "Billy" Kyles has served as pastor of Monumental Baptist Church in Memphis since 1959 and has served on the Board of Directors of Morehouse School of Religion. Having participated in many of the civil rights struggles throughout the South, Rev. Kyles is recognized as an important resource on the Civil Rights Movement.

Portia Wills Lee is Senior Pastor of Trinity African Baptist Church in Mableton, Georgia. Her pioneering leadership within the American Baptist Convention has been nationally noted and Trinity is the first church, headed by a woman pastor, to join the New Era State Convention. Her community and civic activities have earned her numerous leadership awards, including Woman of the Year, 2000 of Concerned Black Clergy of Atlanta. She serves as an advisor to seminary students at the Candler School of Theology.

Vashti M. McKenzie was elected the 117th and first female Bishop of the African Methodist Episcopal Church. She is president of the Council of Bishops of the AME Church and Presiding Prelate of the Thirteenth Episcopal District. She served with distinction over the 18th District in South Africa and holds the position of Chaplain of the Delta Sigma Theta Sorority. Her publications include *Journey to the Well* and *Not without a Struggle.*

OTIS MOSS JR. is Senior Pastor of Olivet Institutional Baptist Church in Cleveland. He is a renowned preacher, community activist, and religious leader. He has delivered sermons and lectures throughout the world. A friend and associate of Dr. Martin Luther King Jr., he serves on the board of the Martin Luther King Jr. Center for Non-Violent Social Change.

OTIS MOSS III is senior pastor of the Historic Tabernacle Baptist Church in Augusta, Georgia. He has done extensive research in the areas of African American culture, theology and youth development. He has published many articles, poetry and *Redemption in a Red Light District*. The African American Pulpit named him as one of the "20 to watch" who will shape the future of the African American church.

LARRY MURPHY is Professor of History of Christianity and Director of the PhD Program at Garrett Evangelical Theological Seminary in Evanston, Illinois. He is the author and editor of several articles and publications, including *African-American Faith in America*, *Encyclopedia of World Religions*, and *Down By the Riverside: Readings in African American Religion*.

CECIL L. "CHIP" MURRAY is Pastor Emeritus of First African Methodist Church in Los Angeles. His work in urban ministry is legendary. He has lectured and been adjunct professor at Iliff School of Theology, Seattle University, School of Theology at Claremont, Fuller Theological Seminary, and Northwest Theological Seminary.

RENITA J. WEEMS is the William and Camille Olivia Hanks Cosby Endowed Professor at Spelman College in Atlanta and serves as Professor of Hebrew Bible at Vanderbilt University Divinity School. She is the author of many scholarly articles and several widely acclaimed books on women's spirituality and wholeness including *Just a Sister Away*, *I Asked for Intimacy*, *Listening for God*, and *Showing Mary*.

REGINALD WILLIAMS is Associate Pastor for Justice Ministries at Trinity United Church of Christ in Chicago. "Rev. Reggie" provides spiritual support, guidance, and assistance for the thirteen ministries within Trinity's Christian Education Division of Justice. Also trained as a lawyer, he has been instrumental in organizing models for justice ministries locally, nationally, and internationally.

GAYRAUD WILMORE is Professor Emeritus of African American Church History at the Interdenominational Theological Center and Editor Emeritus of the *Journal of the Interdenominational Theological Center*. Wilmore has written and edited over sixteen books including *Black Religion and Black Radicalism: An Interpretation of the Religious History of African Americans and his latest publication, Pragmatic Spirituality*.

JEREMIAH A. WRIGHT JR. is Senior Pastor of Trinity United Church of Christ in Chicago and an internationally renowned preacher. As an interdisciplinary scholar and teacher, he has also lectured throughout the world. He has authored several volumes, including *When Black Men Stand Up for God, Good News! Sermons of Hope for Today's Families, Africans Who Shaped Our Faith*, and *What Makes You So Strong?*

Preface

Dwight N. Hopkins

Roughly one hundred years ago, one of the major intellectual and activist giants of the African American community stood at the crossroads between the end of the nineteenth century and the beginning of the twentieth. He pondered the difficult efforts to sing our ancestors' songs in a strange land. And so he surveyed our history: our journey from great civilizations on the West Coast of Africa; through our holocaust and Maafa during the European slave trade in black bodies, including the forced arrival of seventeen African men and three African women to Jamestown, Virginia, in August 1619; through the slavery period, the end of chattel oppression, and the rise and fall of Reconstruction; into the rituals of late-nineteenth-century "black codes," lynching and segregation, and the spiritual resistance displayed in the pre-1865, northern African independent churches and the underground African Christian churches during slavery; to the pioneering efforts of the Black church–influenced women's club movements and the global pan-African conferences. With this historical sweep, William Edward Burghardt (W. E. B.) DuBois stood at the dawn of the 1900s and proclaimed that the essential issue for America in the twentieth century would be the question of the color line.

Today, as we stand at the crossroads of the end of the twentieth century and the start of the twenty-first century, we too can look back over the past one hundred years and agree with DuBois that, yes indeed, the color line has been the fundamental characteristic of American culture and religion in the twentieth century.

The unpaid labor of our enslaved African and African American foreparents built this country. For over two hundred years, Black Christian field-workers, house chattel, and skilled workers gave their blood, sweat, and tears to make white (Christian) Americans gain free wealth and privileges. From 1865 to 1965, our mothers and fathers worked on railroads, as tenant farmers, and in Ms. Ann's kitchen; they nursed babies, chopped down trees for new developments, worked on chain gangs, toiled in steel mills, auto factories, and coal mines throughout this land—all during a period of legal and state-sponsored segregation, which was nothing but another form of white Christian apartheid. Even with the end of legal segregation, symbolized by the 1964 Civil Rights Bill and the 1965 Voting Rights Act, African American people continued to endure structural and personal forms of discrimination.

Still, today, at the crossroads of the twenty-first century, we can look back and see that there have been some advancements for our people. We have civil rights and voting rights, we have freedom of movement and access to housing, we have medical and legal avenues, we have educational and job opportunities, and we have free religious expression. And some of us even have the right to become part of the black bourgeoisie. In one sense, we, the people of African descent— sojourners in Babylon—have met DuBois's challenge of the color line in the twentieth century.

Yet I think that if the greatest son of the Black church were alive today, he would further challenge us with another agenda for the twenty-first century. If the Rev. Dr. Martin Luther King Jr. were among us, he would turn his gaze from the civil rights victories of the last century and urge us to continue the struggle around the color line. But I think he would broaden DuBois's poignant observation. Preacher King would say that the defining characteristics of American culture and religion now are the plight and prospects of the poor, especially the African American poor.

In his pastoral, priestly, and prophet roles, King announced clearly that God's call to people of faith is to set the captives free. And especially toward the end of his ministry, he argued that Bible-based Christianity and our ancestors' traditions move us to see that the overwhelming captives among us are Black working-class people and those in structural poverty. That is why King began to raise questions like, In a world made of two-thirds water, why do we have to pay for water bills? and Who owns the iron ore, steel, and oil? That is why Dr. King dedicated his calling and ultimately gave his life for a Poor People's Campaign.

But, unlike King, we have bought into the falsehoods of American popular thinking. For instance, one of the biggest lies propagated by the powerful in the U.S.A. is to have us only focus on equal opportunity to achieve equal income with white folks. We can never be truly free if we stop at equal opportunity. At the crossroads of the twenty-first century, we must now include the prophetic agenda of creating equal conditions to achieve equal wealth. Equal opportunity to attain income is a fight to have the right for someone else to pay us money. But equal conditions to attain wealth is a struggle for poor people to control the wealth of this land. There is a huge difference between income and wealth. God's call today is for the Black church to stand in the gap for the rights of the materially poor and emotionally bruised to own and share in the wealth of this nation. Any fair-minded person can see that from 1619 to this very moment, despite all the achievements Black folk have made, the gulf between who owns wealth and who does not has widened. In fact, today the United States is undergoing one of the biggest redistributions of wealth in the history of the nation. Unfortunately, it is a redistribution upwards.

And it is not simply a matter of materialism or acquiring more "stuff." It is fundamentally a theological question. It is a question of our faith. Indeed, this is why King ended his ministry working on a Poor People's Campaign and supporting Black garbage laborers. King eventually concluded that the poor and working-class folk symbolize the presence of Jesus Christ among us. King started to reread the Bible with new eyes. He found the driving force in the Old Testament was freedom for slaves. The Exodus narrative is not about the middle class or the bourgeoisie. Leaving the fleshpots of captivity is about liberating working people. And through them, all humanity would be free. The emancipation of the Hebrew people would be a sign that Yahweh can defeat Satan and will surely deliver all women and men.

Furthermore, King studied the New Testament and discovered Luke 4:18-19—the Holy Spirit has anointed the followers of the faith. Likewise, the Reverend Dr. King read the entire Word of God and discerned that the only passage in the Holy Bible that gives instructions on how to get into heaven is in Matt. 25:31-46—the story of the "Son of Man" separating the sheep from the goats. One day when we all cross over Jordan, Jesus will ask us what we did for the poor. And based on our relation to setting the poor free, we will be free to enter heaven as sheep of the Shepherd, or we will be turned away as selfish goats.

To be able one day to hear the Savior say, "Well done, my faithful servant," the challenge for today's Black church is to help lead a new struggle in King's and Fannie Lou Hamer's tradition. It is a spiritual struggle to transform the soul of America from the demons of me-first, self-interests, and stepping on the necks of society's vulnerable. Moreover, these demons increase privatization by those who monopolize the nation's wealth. But all that we see are creations of God. The air that we breathe, the land that we walk on, all the resources of this nation belong to God. In the words of Dr. King, how can something created by and belonging to God become privately owned by roughly two hundred white families in America? The U.S. system of monopoly capitalism is one of the greatest abominations since the Tower of Babel and Sodom and Gomorrah. That is why, from a theological perspective, the Black church is at a crossroads today. But the Lord be praised! God has not given up on us. God is still calling us to set the captives free—not only for the heavy-hearted, the hopeless, and the helpless—but for our own individual spiritual health.

That is why, if we each believe that Jesus Christ is our personal Lord and Savior, the Black church needs to help build a national movement for a Poor People's Bill of Rights. To radically change the spiritual demon of privatized and monopolized wealth, we need to witness in this world.

If we do not take up the challenge for this century, this decade, this year, and this month, Black folk in Africa, Asia, the Caribbean, Latin America, and the Pacific Islands and our ancestors, our children, and our unborn will be a witness against us. Yet, like King, I have rock-solid faith that just as Jesus made a way out of no way for our foreparents, he will never—no, not ever—leave us alone. If we follow his path, even though we may not get to a new society in our lifetime, God has sent the Holy Spirit as a promise that our children and our children's children will reap the benefits of our efforts. Let us be faithful to God's call and blow the trumpet in Zion!

Acknowledgments

THIS VOLUME IS POSSIBLE because a few of God's people answered the call to solemn assembly of a charter gathering of the Samuel DeWitt Proctor Conference on February 10–12, 2004. We are grateful to all who assembled. The dynamism, power, and spirit of that assembly can never be fully captured by the written word. However, the piercing critiques, history, and celebration reflected in this collection of documents represent a vision and a charge for future generations in the African American church.

Selected presentations from the conference have been enveloped by and woven within historical and prospective essays to tell a story and chart a course. We are grateful to all of these contributors for their intellectual and spiritual gifts. We are also grateful to all who presented at the conference to make it the anointed assembly that it was, including those whose contributions are not represented in this volume.

We the editors, along with others, shared the vision to give life to this charter gathering and to position the telling of its story as a part of the ongoing legacy of the African American church. Rev. Ron Bonner, Manager of Multicultural Resources at Augsburg Fortress, must be credited with seeing beyond the moment and envisioning a written work such as this. He, along with Michael West, editor-in-chief of Fortress Press, immediately and wholeheartedly embraced this project. This book would not have been possible without the dedicated support of Katara Washington. It was Katara's sensibilities and skills that kept the editing process moving as we threaded the pieces. We also appreciate the support from Fortress Press staff, Jessica Thoreson, managing editor, and Becky Lowe, production editor.

Finally, we are profoundly grateful to our other trustees who have joined us to initiate, grow, and sustain the Samuel DeWitt Proctor Conference. We look forward to this being the first of a series that will continue to write the vision and make it plain.

IVA E. CARRUTHERS
FREDERICK D. HAYNES III
JEREMIAH A. WRIGHT JR.

I

Sent to Proclaim Release to the Captives

1.

The Continuing Legacy
of Samuel DeWitt Proctor

Jeremiah A. Wright Jr.

Dr. Samuel DeWitt Proctor has been more than a fixture in my life for over five decades. Dr. Proctor has been more than the magnetic North Pole, which he described in one of his best "sermonic stories" about the magnetic pull on a compass that has been buried beneath the soil and the muck and the mire of life's tragic, unfortunate, and ugly experiences.

Sam used to love to point out that whenever that compass was dug up, unearthed, and released from its prison of impossibilities, there was a God-created pull that would always cause the needle on the compass to point toward that which God created—no matter how deep the burial, how dark the imprisonment, or how long the imprisonment. Sam Proctor was like that North Pole pull in my life!

From the days of my childhood, in my home there were always stories about Sam Proctor and the Proctor family. Dr. Proctor was a member of and grew up in the Bank Street Baptist Church of Norfolk, Virginia. My mother's oldest brother, Dr. John B. Henderson, was the pastor of Bank Street throughout my childhood, my youth, and my young adult years.

When I was in high school, Dr. Proctor became the president of Virginia Union University. During my "turbulent" years (my adolescence), Dr. Samuel DeWitt Proctor's name and persona became a permanent part of my personality, my personal development, my ministerial identity, and my understanding of the Christian faith as an African American living in the bowels of white racism and segregation.

My family's history with Virginia Union University went back to the late 1800s, and Dr. Proctor was the president of the school that shaped my family for over half a century. My grandparents, Dr. Hamilton Martin Henderson and Mrs. Mamie Hamlet Henderson, were both graduates of Virginia Union. My grandfather finished Waylend Seminary and my grandmother finished Hartshorn College before those two schools merged to become Virginia Union. My grandfather received a BTh, a BA, and his MDiv from Virginia Union. My parents, Dr. Jeremiah A. Wright Sr. and Dr. Mary Henderson Wright met at and both graduated from Virginia Union. My mother received her BA from Virginia Union. My father received a BTh, a BA, and his MDiv from Virginia Union. Their meeting at Virginia Union led to their marriage a month after they graduated in 1938. My uncles, John, Thomas, and Welton, were also graduates of Virginia Union, and I was headed for that historically Black university from the time I was in my mother's womb!

Three and a half months after I turned eighteen, I was a freshman at Virginia Union University, and I got to know Samuel DeWitt Proctor "up close and personal" in a way most college students today never dream of knowing the presidents of the colleges and universities they attend.

On one of his many trips to Philadelphia to raise money for the university, Dr. Proctor asked me if I wanted a ride home to see my parents for the weekend. I said, "Yes." I grabbed a bag full of dirty clothes to be washed by my mother while I was at home for the weekend, and we took off on a five-and-a-half-hour car trip from Richmond, Virginia, to Philadelphia, Pennsylvania. Dr. Proctor took advantage of that five and a half hours to teach me my first lesson in homiletics.

For five and a half hours he explained the Hegelian method of dialectical thinking, reasoning, and arguing. He explained his adaptation of the Hegelian method of thesis, antithesis, and synthesis, and he illustrated with biblical text after biblical text how his method worked by starting off with the antithesis, raising the relevant question, and then proceeding to answer that question (stating both the thesis and the synthesis) in response to the relevant question. He then gave me several texts (from memory!) and made me use his methodology in addressing those texts while we rode from Richmond to Philadelphia.

I had entered Virginia Union University in January of 1959. I accepted my call to ministry in the spring of 1959, and I preached my trial sermon on the first Sunday of May in 1959. By the fall of that year, Dr. Proctor was determined to teach me how to preach using the "Proctor

Method" so that my sermons would (1) make sense to those who heard them, (2) be faithful in exegeting the text historically and contemporaneously, and (3) speak to the heads and the hearts of listeners while addressing the reality of being Black in America in the 1960s.

Please remember: this was happening to me in the years of my "turbulent teens." I was eighteen years old; I was a college freshman and sophomore. This was my first time away from home. This was during the period of my life when I was exposed (for the first time) to the underside (or the seedy side) of the Black church and hypocritical Black preachers.

My father was a Black preacher, but my father was "cut from the same cloth" as my maternal grandfather, my uncle, John B. Henderson, and my mentor, Samuel DeWitt Proctor. My father did not drink. He did not smoke cigarettes. He did not chase women, and he was a seminary graduate.

I soon discovered that my dad and my mother's dad, my mother's brothers, and Dr. Proctor were the glowing "exceptions to the rule" when it came to Black preachers in America in the late 1950s and the early 1960s. That was a turbulent time for me!

The Civil Rights Movement was in full swing in 1959 and 1960. I was a part of the student sit-in movement of 1960 and 1961. I saw white Christian racism up close and "in my face" as a freshman and sophomore in college—all while pledging the fraternity of my father, Omega Psi Phi, and singing as a soloist in the traveling university choir, getting drunk for the first time in my life, and trying to sort out my call to ministry, God's call upon my life, and the "honkies" I was growing to hate with each passing day. That was a turbulent time for me!

All throughout this time, however, there was Sam Proctor, the "North Star pull" upon the compass of my life. Sam Proctor was always there, and Sam Proctor was always pointing me to a higher calling and a deeper commitment to a faith grounded in a carpenter from Capernaum who knew oppression, who knew hatred, who knew colonialism, but who also knew (personally) a God who was greater than any government and who promised a peace more powerful than any peace the "world" could ever give.

For me, trying to describe the continuing importance of Dr. Proctor's legacy is like trying to describe the splendor of God's creation (as articulated in the eighth Psalm) or trying to describe the relationship between air and breathing. I will take a stab at it, however, based on my forty years of an intimate relationship with the man whose ministry changed my life.

Dr. Proctor, in the closing years of his pastoral ministry, taught his students to categorize their thoughts in broad brush strokes. He was fond of saying that he had four "main arrows" in his homiletical quiver that he could identify after sixty-plus years of ministry.

Using Sam's paradigm, I would like to address the four arrows in the quiver of his legacy that every serious student of his needs to study. Those arrows are (1) intellectual excellence, (2) cultural relevance, (3) spiritual or theological integrity; and (4) social honesty.

Intellectual Excellence

The intellectual excellence that Sam Proctor demanded was an excellence that mirrored his own mental makeup. Dr. Proctor never asked his students to be anything more than what God created them to be.

He believed in people, and he believed any student who had made it to Virginia Union, North Carolina A&T, or Rutgers University had the intellectual ability to complete the program they started, whether it was an undergraduate program or a PhD program. (At Sam's funeral the president of Rutgers University pointed out that Sam had single-handedly produced more African American PhDs at Rutgers than any other person in the history of the school.)

Dr. Proctor wanted all of his students to do as he had done, which is to take what they had been given by their life experiences and their academic exposure and make something special in their chosen profession that would be a blessing to the generations coming after them. What Sam was given and what Sam was exposed to made Sam who he was intellectually, and who he was intellectually was absolutely incredible.

Sam Proctor was raised in a climate of academic excellence. Not only was the life of the mind important in the Proctor household in Norfolk, Virginia, but critical thinking and mental acuity were enhanced (his parents believed) by the mastery of musical instruments. Each child in the Proctor household had to learn how to play a musical instrument.

Add to his family-of-origin experience the Bank Street Baptist Church experience, and you catch a glimpse of the next factor that shaped what I am calling Sam's paradigm for academic and intellectual excellence. At the Bank Street Baptist Church, where Sam grew up, he was in an atmosphere of African American professionals who showed him by their lives and their service that there was no contradiction between the life of the mind and the love of the Lord.

At Bank Street Church, physicians sang in the choir and school principals served with the Sunday School. At Bank Street Church,

Sam was as likely to see his math teacher from the school he attended as he was to see his next-door neighbor.

Sam's mental makeup, however, was influenced not only by his family life and his home church but also by the giants he encountered at Virginia Union University. Long before he got to Crozier Theological Seminary or Boston University (where he earned his doctorate), Sam was influenced by Pat McGuin and Gordon Blaine Hancock in sociology and anthropology; these Virginia Union faculty members demonstrated to Sam academic excellence at its finest. Gordon Blaine Hancock—a Harvard graduate—also pastored the Moore Street Baptist Church around the corner from Virginia Union University.

John Malcus Ellison was one of many mentors at Virginia Union who also helped to shape Sam's mental makeup. Arthur Davis and Sterling Brown were two other giants who rubbed up against Sam's personality and helped to hone his worldview. Arthur Davis, Sterling Brown, and Ulysses Lee edited the groundbreaking volume *The Negro Caravan*, and their writings (and thoughts) were a part of Sam Proctor's mental makeup.

Sterling Brown, of course, was not only a professor. He was also a poet, a product of the Harlem Renaissance, which with its giants fed into the intellectual landscape across which Sam Proctor's life traveled. Zora Neale Hurston, Langston Hughes, Claude McKay, and Jean Toomer were names that Sam knew just as he knew the names of Isaac Watts, France Jane (Fanny) Crosby, and James Weldon Johnson.

The writings of W. E. B. DuBois and the scholarship of William Leo Hansberry both influenced Sam's thinking, and in my many conversations with him, I could hear the workings of a brilliant mind shaped by a providential mixture of personalities, disciplines, movements, art, and scholarship that was absolutely breathtaking.

Sam didn't think he was anything "special," however. He believed all of his students could master everything that he had mastered, and it was on the basis of that belief that Sam demanded intellectual excellence.

Cultural Relevance

A second piece of the continuing legacy that Sam Proctor left us is the importance of cultural relevance. Sam was not in the age group (or of the mind-set) of younger African Americans who started to wear dashikis and Afros back in the 1960s, but Sam was at the epicenter of the cultural revolution and cultural awakening taking place as African Americans began to reclaim their connection to the continent of Africa.

As an outside observer, I would guess that a combination of factors led to Sam's perspective on and his commitment to the people of Africa and people of African descent. That combination would include his growing up through the Marcus Garvey years and experiencing Garvey's Back to Africa movement, the influence of the Harlem Renaissance and its identification with and celebration of Africa, his immersion in the Lott Carey Foreign Mission family (both at Bank Street and as a Virginia Baptist), his passion for helping African students through their undergraduate and MDiv studies at Virginia Union University, and his association with people like W. E. B. Du-Bois, William Leon Hansberry, and Kwame Nkrumah.

Those are my observations as to what caused Sam to be at the center of the cultural revolution and cultural "awakening" that took place back in the 1960s. Whether my observations are accurate, the fact remains that Sam Proctor said yes to Sargent Shriver and took an assignment as the head of the Peace Corps in Nigeria, and he served there for six years. Adding to his wealth of knowledge concerning Liberian and Ghanaian culture, Sam had six years of experience in Nigeria serving the Ibo, the Ibibio, and the Yoruban people, learning from their culture and drinking deep from the wells of their wisdom.

Sam's training as a Christian minister and his widely disparate experiences at Bank Street, Virginia Union University, Crozier Theological Seminary, and Boston University (during the years of segregation, Jim Crow, racism, and the Civil Rights Movement—including the student sit-ins while he was president of Virginia Union University and North Carolina A&T) created a canvas onto which was painted his Nigerian experience. Once again, that providential mixture gave Sam a perspective on cultural relevancy that was both revolutionary and refreshing.

Dr. Proctor taught that the gospel we preach could not be cut off from the culture that produced it or the culture that produced us. That part of the Proctor legacy becomes extremely important in an age of "prosperity preachers," who operate as if we live in a cultural vacuum. The garbage being proclaimed as the gospel by the prosperity pimps preaches capitalism as being synonymous with Christianity. It also preaches the philosophy of Adam Smith as if Smith's philosophy were the theology of an almighty Savior!

Capitalism as made manifest in the "New World" depended upon slave labor (by African slaves), and it is only maintained by keeping the "Two-Thirds World" under oppression. That heresy has nothing to do with the message of the man from Galilee, a Capernaum carpenter who had no place to lay his head, and that heresy is completely oblivious of the culture that produced the gospel and the culture of Africans living in the American diaspora.

Dr. Proctor taught that cultural relevance is crucial if we are to be faithful to the gospel of Jesus Christ instead of being faithful to the gospel of Adam Smith. We are descendants of Africa, not England. We have a culture that is not English. We are descendants of Africa, not Europe. We have a culture that is African in origin—not European. The Bible we preach came from a culture that was not English or European. Rightly dividing the Word of Truth means taking seriously the culture that produced that Word.

When the Word became flesh to dwell among us, the Word did not come from eternity into time in England or Europe. The "scandal of specificity" means that God became human in a specific place, in a specific culture, and among a specific people. Those people were neither English nor European, and failure to come to grips with that is to miss the message completely and to take it out of context totally.

Spiritual Integrity

Both on the personal level and on the professional level, Sam Proctor leaves us a legacy of spiritual and theological integrity. On the personal level, as the old folks would put it, "There was no gap between his 'talk and his walk'!"

With all of the scandals in the media concerning the clergy (beginning in the 1990s), there was never any fear in anyone's heart about a scandal surfacing that would involve Samuel DeWitt Proctor. He was not that kind of man. He was not that kind of preacher.

Sam lived the life he preached about, and we are forever in his debt because of his impeccable personal integrity. Sam believed that God had given the calling of clergy a special blessing, and he believed that it was incumbent upon all who said yes to that call to "walk worthy" of the profession into which they had entered.

He loved to tell us how his mother "ruined" his notions of a night out on the town. While in college, Sam came home for one of the holidays, and he had a night of "manly mischief" all planned out. He put on extra cologne as he checked his dapper wardrobe. He stepped out of his bedroom on his way out into the night as a Kappa man about to enjoy the evening and whatever the evening brought.

When he reached the first floor and was headed for the front door, his mother called him into the room where she was. She inspected his attire. She straightened his tie, and she said to him, "Don't forget: Wherever you go tonight and whatever you do tonight, you are a Proctor!"

Those words and that reminder made him go back upstairs, pull his dapper clothes off, and go to bed! That family story, however, became a faith paradigm for the way Sam lived his life as a minister of the gospel.

He never forgot that wherever he went and whatever he did, he was a preacher of the gospel! His calling demanded a level of integrity beyond reproach, and he fulfilled his calling on the personal level. Spiritual integrity was a sine qua non for Sam Proctor.

On the professional level, theological integrity was just as important for him. No matter what new things he learned—at Virginia Union University, at Crozier, or at Boston University—he did not give up on the Jesus he had met at Bank Street Baptist Church or in his home in Norfolk, Virginia. No matter what powerful teachings he experienced—from DuBois, Hansberry, African culture, or nineteenth-century German higher biblical criticism—he did not let those teachings cause him to let go of the nail-pierced hand of the man who had stilled the storm on the Sea of Galilee. He maintained his theological integrity.

Sam told the first group of Proctor Fellows at United Theological Seminary in Dayton, Ohio, that he had to "put his Bible back together" when he got out of seminary. The seminary professors had torn it to shreds with biblical criticism and archaeological findings, and he was not sure what to believe or what to preach when they finished. He had to put it back together to maintain theological integrity.

But then Sam also told the fellows that the year 1957 literally "rocked his world." Not only were the Civil Rights demonstrations going on in 1957, not only was his friendship with "Mike" (Dr. Martin Luther King) pushing his understanding of the Christian faith (in the context of North American Christian hypocrisy) to the limit, but in 1957 the Russians launched a satellite named Sputnik. That launch disrupted Sam's entire understanding of the Bible, God, Jesus, and heaven.

All his life, Sam had been taught that heaven was up and that hell was down, but with the launch of Sputnik, he found out that there was no "up" and there was no "down." There was only "out there"! The earth was hurtling through space, and there was no such thing as "up" any longer.

There went the Bible verse of Jesus "ascending *up* into heaven!" (in the book of Acts). There went the notion of heaven as *up*, and there went the understanding that Jesus was *up* in heaven seated at the right hand of God the Father.

Sam was getting ready to retire from Abyssinian Baptist Church as he told us this story, and he said to us (demonstrating his theological integrity), "So I didn't know any more after 1957 where heaven was, and I still don't know where heaven is! But this one thing I do know: When I have pulled off my preaching robe for the last time, when I have laid my Bible down for the last time, and when I stick my sword in the sands of time, *wherever* my Jesus is, that is heaven; and I am going to be with Jesus."

Theological integrity and spiritual integrity are an invaluable part of the legacy that Sam Proctor leaves us, and any student of Sam who tries to walk on the pathway he blazed for us needs to take these pieces of the legacy just as seriously as he or she takes Sam's commitment to intellectual excellence and cultural relevance.

Social Honesty

The experience of being the president of two historically Black universities during the 1950s and 1960s combined with the experience of growing up Black in a world of white racism gave Sam Proctor a perspective on pastoral ministry that was undergirded by what I call social honesty.

There could be no denial of the social setting in which Sam labored and preached, taught and hoped, dreamed and did what God gave him to do. He had to be honest. There could be no pretense about not seeing the arrogance and white supremacy of the white pastor of the First Baptist Church of Richmond, a man to whom the Black presence of Mr. Benjamin Lambert (the caterer) was invisible.

Lambert served the head table where Sam and the white pastor sat. While the white pastor talked to a Black college president, a Black "servant" could not be seen or acknowledged. Sam could not pretend that he did not see that, that it did not affect him, that he was not offended by it. Sam had to be honest!

In the last sermon Dr. Proctor preached (in the pulpit of Trinity United Church of Christ in Chicago, where God has placed me), Sam recounted for us the social reality of trying to prepare for ministry at Crozier Theological Seminary, a racist place, and he recounted for us how God took that negative experience and gave him "beauty for ashes." Sam had to be honest.

He knew that those whom he taught and those whom he served lived in a world where racism was (and is) alive and well. Honesty is needed in a day and age when the "colored hustlers" of TV ministry try to act as if that social reality is a thing of the past. Social honesty is a much-needed hermeneutic in preaching the gospel during "this present age." Without it, we are "lying to the races" and setting the sons and daughters of African descent up for disappointment, disillusionment, and disenchantment with the "God of our weary years."

If we cannot be honest, then we need to turn in our preaching credentials and sell insurance policies or sell swampland in Florida, because we are not being true to the God who has called us and we are not being faithful to the social context that has shaped us.

Harriet Tubman did not risk her life so we can preach about money. Yaa Asantewa did not fight against British oppression in Ghana so we could become a part of the American oppression that keeps Africans in economic bondage.

Sam Proctor did not go through all he went through so we could distort the gospel of Jesus Christ and preach about financial "breakthroughs." The legacy he leaves is not the Prayer of Jabez in blackface. The legacy Sam leaves us is found in the prayer of Jesus, who taught us that whatever we have done to the least of these, we have done unto him.

2.

The Sheep and the Goats
Black and Christian in a Global Context

Iva E. Carruthers

SAMUEL DEWITT PROCTOR, twentieth-century prophet of the Black church, was a scholar, teacher, university president, public servant, Africanist, mentor, family man, and preacher. His life and legacy is a model of uncompromised faithfulness, theological integrity, and informed social action.

The Proctor Conference was born with a claim to represent a paradigm shift reflected by acts of reclamation and proclamation—a reclamation of the spirit of liberation imbued in the life of the African American church and African American Christianity and a proclamation of commitment to confront those present forms of gross injustice apparent at the beginning of the twenty-first century. These injustices are widening, becoming more entrenched, institutionalized, and apparent under the movement of globalized capitalism and Kingdom Theology. A few are getting richer, and the poor are getting poorer. Ignorance of the facts can no longer be an excuse for inaction; the Black church is called to respond.

Computer and biogenetic technological advances and capacity during the last half of the twentieth century have completely transformed the possibilities for human community. Information can be stored, transmitted, and retrieved in the world's electronic village, the Internet. Human genetic cloning is on the horizon. Yet, despite such advances, the gap between those who control these technologies and those who do not, "the least of these," is widening, creating a huge difference in quality of life throughout the world. This is especially true of Africa, where the embryonic developmental stages of newly independent nations and their quests for stability are falling prey to a complex of issues, including the legacy of colonialism, unmerited debt to the West, political corruption, and the HIV/AIDS pandemic. With the double-edged sword of being the least among those who have the most, to be African American and also to be Christian in the twenty-first century is to be uniquely challenged and positioned in the world to heed the call of Jesus.

The maturity and faithfulness of the African American church in the twenty-first century will be judged not by how large or prosperous it is, but by the simple parable of the sheep and the goats: "for I was hungry and you gave me food, I was thirsty and you gave me something to drink, I was a stranger and you welcomed me, I was naked and you gave me clothing, I was sick and you took care of me, I was in prison and you visited me" (Matt. 25:35-36). This is the mandate for twenty-first-century ministry in the global context.

From a Christian perspective, justice for African Americans and setting the captives free in the United States has always been inextricably connected to global justice and liberating the poor throughout the world. This is not an *either/or* paradigm; it is a divine paradigm that is *both/and*. And no group of persons is more equipped as earthly and celestial witnesses on the side of the God of righteousness than the African remnant of God's people, who continue to navigate and survive the vicissitudes of dehumanization in the crucible of white supremacy and racism, U.S.A. style.

The very nature of white supremacy and racism in America is systemically global in its reach. Thus, the quest for freedom, equality, and justice for African Americans has always had a global dimension. First and foremost, African Americans find themselves in a three-hundred-year protracted quest for freedom, equality, and justice because they were snatched from their homelands by a European state- and church-led system of international slave trafficking. Second, for over three centuries African Americans have been subject to and sought remedy through international solutions, including official U.S. expatriation schemes, for example, Haiti and Liberia, and legal arguments for reparations placed before the international courts and the United Nations. Last, African American movements for freedom, equality, and justice have been by example a beacon of light and hope that continues to reverberate and energize oppressed peoples throughout the world, from Accra to Soweto to Tiananmen Square.

The progressive wing of the Black church—its theology, its leaders, its pan-African missions, and its peculiar call—has been one of God's instruments by which God's people can judge themselves and be judged on the gospel's call to set the captives free. Now, at the turn of the twenty-first century, at the crossroads, are the people who wear Langston Hughes's "masks that grin and bear," who are bearers of W. E. B. DuBois's "double-edged sword" and "double consciousness," and who pray the prayer of James Weldon Johnson, "Let us be true to our native land."

This revelatory moment will be a historical marker that will determine who we really are and what we really mean when we say we are Black and Christian. The CNN era has ushered into our living rooms a snapshot of the world's oppressed and struggling people. Ignorance can no longer be an excuse, and God is about to cross-examine the emotions of our heart, the depth of our faith, and the content of our character.

A snapshot of God's world from below is compelling:

- The World Bank estimates that 1.1 billion people are poor by an income standard of earning one dollar per day. Thirty million children die of illnesses not typically fatal in high-income nations.
- Five hundred million people are hungry daily.
- In excess of forty-five million people in the world are either international refugees or displaced within the borders of their own country.
- The African continent is experiencing depopulation at pandemic rates, along with attendant human suffering from one end of the continent to the other.
- HIV/AIDS has orphaned some fifteen million children; siphoned off more than 50 percent of the heath budgets of Africa; and reduced the average life span in many African countries by half.
- The African continent is claimed to owe 230 billion Western creditors. This translates to nearly four hundred dollars per capita, more than four times the per capita income.
- Of the world's obsolete pesticides, 20 percent are dumped and stored in Africa.

Juxtapose this snapshot against the crucible of hegemonic power in the world and the country in which the African American church is called to live out its mission.

- The assets of 358 billionaires—largely from the United States but whose citizenship transcends national boundaries—exceed the combined incomes of 45 percent of the world's population.
- Fifty-one of the one hundred largest economies in the world are not countries but multinational corporations with ties to the United States.

- The United States is first in gross domestic product.
- The United States is first in military technology and exports.
- The United States is first in health technology.
- The United States is first in the number of millionaires and billionaires.
- Of the 154 members of the United Nations, the United States is the only country that has failed to ratify the United Nations Convention on the Rights of the Child and the Convention on the Elimination of All Forms of Discrimination against Women. The United States boycotted the 2001 United Nations World Congress against Racism, Racial Discrimination, Xenophobia, and Related Intolerance.
- U.S. policy toward Africa has compelling implications for the African American church. In 2000, despite the spiraling negative conditions afflicting Africa, U.S. aid to Israel—a *country* of about 6 million people—was $3.1 *billion*, while aid to Africa—a *continent* of fifty-four countries and close to 800 million people—received a decreased U.S. package of $760 *million*.

This "prosperous," powerful, and hard-hearted war machine—the United States—is organized to sustain its global hegemony and economic control at any cost and to do so "in the name of God." From Cuba to Haiti to Korea to Iraq, the United States has wielded its power based on principles totally antithetical to the common good.

In 1970 Escott Reid, former president of the World Bank, promoted the eventual crumbling of the wall between the West and the East as a means to maintain European consciousness and control over the rest of the world. That self-fulfilling prophecy has now been actualized with the promotion of a new NATO–Russian partnership, while seven of the former Eastern bloc states have now become members of NATO. And in the wake of the war on terrorism, the United States and NATO forces have now claimed the authority to set up "benevolent watchtowers in the name of democracy" in Africa.

The question becomes: How do African American Christians extricate themselves from this citadel of global demonic hegemony? Or, better, how do we become better agents of deconstruction and transformation? The answer lies in our willingness to become better informed and more participatory in the global village, to become more intentional about our efforts to shape global outcomes, and to demonstrate our convictions of faith and our moral authority courageously by daring to speak truth to power. For the Black church it is the difference between sustaining our legacy as the prophetic church in America or becoming an extension of the state church.

The State Church and Kingdom Theology, the Prophetic Church and Black Theology

With this global reality, this Kairotic moment for the Black church is defined by a clear choice: either to be a state church on the side of humankind, wearing the privileges of global oppression, *or* to be a prophetic church on the side of Jesus, bearing the gospel of liberation. In both symbolic and real terms, the crossroads has two signposts.

The first and most alluring signpost points to footprints on the road taken by the state church. It reveals an African American people exiled in a corrupt and crumbling kingdom, propped up and sustained by foisting increased injustice and hegemony over the rest of the world. The exiled have a few Esthers in the palace, but the majority of the exiled people is considered fringe, obsolescent, and problematic.

On this road the state church celebrates and collaborates with the palace's chief Esthers: a secretary of state, a national security adviser, a Supreme Court justice, and a preordained successor as national pastor—all of whom have Black skin and represent new firsts in African American life in the United States. The end of this road leads to the Esthers, accompanied by a few other "exceptional" African Americans that society will tolerate, sitting at the palace table wearing the privileges of global oppression.

The second signpost leads down the dusty road of the prophetic church. This road also winds through the land of a people exiled in a corrupt and crumbling kingdom, propped up and sustained by foisting increased injustice and hegemony over the rest of the world. However, despite the chief Esthers in the palace being Black-skinned, the prophetic church has a few sentinels with the discernment and spirit of Mordecai and the conviction to blow the trumpet.

These prophetic trumpeters of the ram's horn blow a sound as piercing today as Miles Davis used to make. Their melodies are the eternal and liberating gospel of Jesus. On this road, despite the occupants in the palace, the end leads to standing on the side of a righteous God and seeking a justice for the common good that is globally transformative.

Every church has a theology or theologies. The theology of the state church has its roots in the stances of the Pharisees and Sadducees that contradicted the call of Jesus. Historically, the theology of the state church divinely ordained and financially supported Catholic and Protestant church initiation of the sixteenth-century international slave trade and the depopulation of African states and takeover of their land.

The state church's authority was far-reaching into the eighteenth-century "New World" and the American context of justifying and controlling plantation slavery. It was likewise a living force in twentieth-century apartheid South Africa as the justification for the abominable imperialistic usurpation of land and resources and complete dehumanization of African indigenous peoples. In all cases, the theology of the state church has been and continues to be an undergirding system of religious justification for white supremacy, racism, economic and political imperialism, and violation of basic human liberties and dignities.

Today, the theology of the state is being masked as "Kingdom Theology," in which Africans in the Americas and African peoples on the continent are being duped to participate in their continued subjugation through a theology designed to serve the status quo and maintain the Euro-Western hegemony of the world.

This Kingdom Theology, also called "Dominion Theology," has as a major proponent Bishop Earl Paulk, a conservative evangelical pastor from Atlanta, who has said, "Kingdom Theology is a whole new theology. . . . What we're doing is setting up a network by which we can spread propaganda . . . so that the systems of the world will collapse because of their inability to survive, and what will be left will be a system the church has built." This agenda is to create a "Christian culture that will have dominion over the world."[1] The soteriology and salvation story of Kingdom Theology consist of a claim that the poor and oppressed have been forsaken by God because of their sins and that ecumenical and interfaith engagement are strategies of Satan. Their mission is thus to save the world from these sin-sick souls and Satanic forces.

For the twenty-first century, this theology has indeed reshaped the form but not the essence of the state church. It has reengineered the matter but not the substance or agenda of the state church. Kingdom Theology is an appendage of twenty-first-century racism and white supremacy that now include technological and ecological tyranny, food and agricultural control: Genetically produced "terminator seeds" that will only reproduce one year are sold to poor farmers. Medical protocols and medicines are distributed based on interests of pharmaceutical giants versus the needs of the people. Toxic waste is disproportionately and globally relocated to the continent of Africa. Experimentation in weather manipulation and biogenetic and chemical human research projects are replete throughout Africa.

Kingdom Theology, led by conservative white evangelicals and distributed by para-church mega-ministries, are seducing and proselytizing Africans in the Americas and on the continent. Their "good works" are distributed through a just-in-time satellite media edutainment modality that makes reality the illusion and the pain go away.

Some argue there is no viable alternative to Kingdom Theology and its twenty-first-century ethic. They believe that through a process of trickle-down economics and globalized capitalism, American-led democracy and controlled growth, the world's oppressed and poor will eventually be better off. And in that scheme of things, Christians will have lived out the mandate of Matthew 25.

But the human carnage taking place throughout the world, especially the many nations on the African continent, compels all Christians to open their eyes and confront those systems and peoples who by commission and omission sustain and perpetrate injustices and atrocities upon already impoverished people. Certainly, the historical and ancestral ties of African Americans to Africa further compel Black Christians to stand up and be counted, to speak truth to power with and on behalf of Africa's poor along with the poor of the world.

Black liberation theology is not an option. Black liberation theology is a sacred hermeneutic. And setting captives free throughout the world is a sacred obligation and task. Despite unparalleled and protracted attempts to break the mind, body, and soul of a people, African Americans are still here, firmly rooted at the crossroads of the twenty-first century in the historical trajectory of the United States. The Black church, at this historical juncture, can either be a voice for global justice or choose to abandon its divine opportunity and its yet untold legacy as an instrument for global transformation.

By expanding and creating new centers of spiritual, knowledge, and material exchange between Africans living on the home continent and Africans of the diaspora, by strengthening and creating new world alliances for global justice, the Black church can lead the world to justice. Globalization of justice, not "Wal-Martization" of the world's economies, is on the side of Jesus.

Ubuntu: A Theological and Ethical Vision for the Twenty-First Century

African Americans have survived in the belly of the beast. There is a divine imperative upon African American Christians to participate in the future role of Christianity in Africa and throughout the world as a part of twenty-first-century global transformation. Beyond the redemptive ancestral calls from the oceans and graves of our people, the shared interests, histories, and specific theological intersections of African peoples and African Americans shape this special purpose. Given the past and the present, we are uniquely positioned to make a difference. The truth of the matter is that:

1. Africa is the crucible of early Christianity. Eden, Egypt, Ethiopia and Punt, the Pishon, Gihon, the Tigris and Euphrates Rivers, and scores of biblical peoples are all on the African continent and can be referred to biblically, as inclusive as the Edenic civilization or as complex and historical as the Egypto-Sudanic civilizations.

2. The epicenter of Christianity has moved from Europe and America to Africa and Asia. This twenty-first-century opportunity for African American and African religious encounters brings new challenges and possibilities for engagement. Conditions and terms of this engagement are neither unrelated to nor missed by the hegemonic interests in Africa on the part of the conservative political and evangelical communities of Europe and the United States. Hopefully, the African American church will not miss these divine opportunities.

3. African traditional religions and diasporic traditions, such as Santeria or Candomblé, continue to incubate and intersect with Euro-Western Christianity. They represent resistant and independent religious expression that at best accommodates Euro-Western forms of Christianity while retaining its African essence. Interfaith dialogue and people-to-people exchange is where ministry lives—not in a closeted and fearful environment of safe havens.

4. African American religious expression, even in its diversity and accommodation of Euro-Western theology, from Pentecostalism to Black Catholicism, has been substantially an expression of hope and liberation from external oppression through and with retention of African cultural essence. Healing from external oppression and deconstruction of internal oppression begin with affirming one's African identity.

These historical and contemporary realities challenge Christians, in general, and African American Christians, in particular, to envision practical possibilities for engendering new forms of lived community in the twenty-first century.

All religion is contextual within sociopolitical and economic spheres. In the face of new forms and systems of oppression, and from the very crucible of global hegemonic oppression, Black Christians in the United States are called to act.

Interfaith and ecumenical engagement with Africa and the rest of the world affords both opportunity and obligation to embrace and engender a transformative and theological ethic. A people without a vision will perish. And a vision outside of God's will is sure to perish. What then becomes a Matthew 25 vision for the world that shapes the peculiar call and global praxis for the African American church in the twenty-first century?

Not surprising, the answer for such a universal and pan-African ethic can be found in the African ontological, theological, and sociological construct of *Ubuntu.*

Ubuntu, as defined by Nelson Mandela—"the profound African sense that we are human only through the humanity of other human beings—is not a parochial phenomenon, but has added globally to our common search for a better world."[2]

In her book on spiritual resilience in South Africa, Linda Thomas writes:

> As a measurable outcome, Ubuntu is assured through accountable relationships identified by the proper offering to the community of goods that are concrete (money, food, housing) and intangible (love, support, care). When harmony exists, these goods move in an uninterrupted circular fashion that flows and crisscrosses with other circles among the living and between the living and the ancestors.[3]

Ubuntu, in principal an operative manifestation of relational and community theology, is in stark opposition to the era and spirit of entitlement that has for centuries undergirded the state church and Euro-Western systems of oppression and white supremacy. The spirit of entitlement has historically led one way—to the lineality of hierarchical privilege, manifested by racism, colorism, classism, and sexism and euphemistically defined by the era and spirit of enlightenment. The era and spirit of Ubuntu call forth a circularity of goodness and operational practices of beneficent distribution of basic human needs and rights and are grounded in principles for the common good.

Without question, Ubuntu can be the foundation for new theological, socioeconomic, and political models to deconstruct and transform the system of entitlement during the twenty-first century. It is not the sole purview of any one group or by the inherited chances of one's race, ethnicity, gender, national origin, or religion to effect this vision. This charge is for all of God's people who want to stand on the side of the God of righteousness and justice.

In his 1967 Christmas Sermon on peace, Dr. Martin Luther King Jr. said: "If we are to have peace on earth, our loyalties must become ecumenical. . . . Our loyalties must transcend our race, our tribe, our class, and our nation. . . . No individual can live alone; no nation can live alone. . . . We must either learn to live together as brothers or we are all going to perish together as fools."[4] Despite the history and contemporary reality of our peoples in Africa and the Americas, it is indeed unfortunate that so many African American church leaders, celebrities, and individuals with access to the media have yet to grasp Dr. King's clarity of position on the interdependence of the quest for justice in America and the quest for justice in the rest of the world. The value of protracted pan-African activism, theologically, politically, and economically, is similarly missed.

You often hear the comments "I ain't left nothing in Africa," "We ought to focus on oppression and injustice down the street instead of in Africa," and "America may have problems, but it is *better than anywhere else in the world.*" On the opposite side of the coin you may hear indigenous Africans say, "I don't understand why African Americans cannot do better." "They don't appreciate what they have."

In both cases, these myopic views are ultimately safe positions from which to avoid the Great Commission as a Christian and to be entrenched as participant beneficiaries of a global and monopolistic capitalism that can only be fueled by global unjust and gross intentional systems of oppression and repression. In short, these views represent a safe harbor for those who want an equal seat at the table of entitlement despite the nature of the sacrificial offerings that comprise the feast.

Black and Christian theologians and pastors are called to preach and pronounce the hermeneutical imperative against racial, gender, class, and technological injustice. Black and Christian congregations are called to continue in the tradition of those who were empowered in the quest for justice by God's liberating and hopeful words of faith, action, and salvation. Black and Christian people are called to use their minds to deconstruct those systems of oppression that bind the threads of Western hegemony, resulting in fewer than 20 percent of the world's population controlling global resources, thus disenfranchising the other 80 percent, largely people of color.

Black and Christian people in America will be increasingly challenged by the stark realities of what's going on in the world to wake up every morning and look in the mirror and hear the voice of Jesus ask, "Who do you say that I am? And whose interest will you serve today?"

This is a Kairos time to stand on the promise of God that—despite an exiled situation—"I will bless you . . . so that you will be a blessing" to others (Gen. 12:2). Our authority emanates from our status as a remnant of divine grace who has been commanded to be a witness unto the ends of the earth. To witness is to testify, advocate, and demand what is right; it is also to testify, advocate, and organize against what is wrong. If there was ever a story of a people wronged, it is the story of Africans of the diaspora, the continent, and their divine relationship to each other.

At the Samuel DeWitt Proctor Conference's call to assembly, I welcomed those gathered in the spirit of a homecoming of a remnant of God's people. We came with conviction to rebuild the walls and renew the energy to fuel our lights of hope and ministries of prophetic witness. As we went forth from the assembly, by reclamation and proclamation, we knew that a prophetic discernment and theological imagination will yield us the capacity to envision what can be in what is, to plant the seeds of possibilities in the legacy soil of ancestral greatness, and to claim the not-yet in the already. Ubuntu, as an ethic of human development and social organization, is a twenty-first-century alternative paradigm to globalized capitalism. Its realization is only limited by our imaginations and our faith.

We who are the greatest witnesses must go forth with a "both/and" spirit of ministry and proclamation to the poor throughout the world. We must be grounded with a vision in our imaginations for Ubuntu, the authority of Jesus' anointing in our spirit, and the Word of God in our hearts. Then, and only then, will we fulfill the divine purpose to be a difference because we made a difference, at home and throughout the world.

3.

From Vision to Action

Principles of Organizing a Theologically Grounded and Vision-Driven Church to Effectively Implement Ministries at the Local, National, and Global Levels

Frederick D. Haynes III

AT THE HEIGHT OF THE CIVIL RIGHTS MOVEMENT IN 1963, the visionary of the "Beloved Community," Martin Luther King Jr., had to wage war on two fronts in Birmingham, Alabama. Not only were the freedom fighters in a battle with the forces of Jim Crow apartheid, Dr. King was attacked by an interdenominational group of ministers who labeled him an outside agitator and questioned the timing of the Birmingham Campaign. This group of ministers published an open letter to Dr. King in the local daily newspaper in Birmingham calling the campaign into question while using the Christian faith as a mask for their desire to maintain a racist status quo. King lovingly and prophetically responded with what came to be known as his "Letter from a Birmingham Jail." In this moving missive he articulated the mission of the Birmingham Movement and his prophetic vision for the nation. He also indicted the church for being the "taillight" as opposed to the "headlight" of the vehicle of society.

His insightful imagery prophetically challenged a church content to sit on the sidelines while being reverent but irrelevant. Taillights on automobiles are colorful and flashy but always behind! Headlights give vision and direction, lead the way, and are most effective in darkness. The local church must recapture and revive its revolutionary role as the headlights in the twenty-first century. A taillight ecclesiology has seduced the church into being inspired but impotent to address the complex challenges that threaten the African American community. This taillight ecclesiology is rooted in an alien theology with a limited concept of spirituality and salvation that energizes parishioners to feel good and make good money but is no good in fulfilling the holistic mission of Jesus Christ. Taillight theology will comfort one's conscience by limiting ministry to acts of charity on life's Jericho Road but will not challenge Pharaoh on issues of injustice to let God's people go. Taillight ecclesiology is really an Americanized version of Christianity that makes Jesus a corporate capitalist while emphasizing individualism, resulting in a church that is concerned not with bearing the cross but with climbing the ladder of success. When Jesus identified his followers as the "light of the world," he surely didn't intend for the church to be the taillights of the world.

It All Begins with Vision

If the Black church is to radically recapture its role as "headlights" in the twenty-first century, it will have to begin with vision. It is not uncommon in the colorful lexicon of the Black church to hear preachers refer to what they can see in their "mind's eye." Or during a sermon they will rhetorically ask for permission to use their "sanctified imagination." Vision may be defined as using one's "sanctified imagination" and "mind's eye" to view the best that is yet to come. Vision may also be defined as a "preview of coming attractions." It is incumbent upon pastoral leadership to use one's sanctified imagination and mind's eye in order to give the congregation something to look forward to. The wisdom writer in the Book of Proverbs declared, "Where there is no vision, the people perish" (Prov. 29:18, King James Version). This passage has also been translated, "Where there is no revelation, the people cast off restraint" (World English Bible). Vision is a revelation of future possibilities that provide direction and discipline.

Our paradigm for perceiving providential possibilities (vision) is rooted in scripture. Nehemiah received word about the devastation and wreckage that the citizens of Jerusalem had grown accustomed to. It is possible to be "down so long until down don't bother" you. The people had adjusted to that which was unsafe and demeaning to their dignity. Nehemiah was blessed with a "good job" as the cupbearer to the king; his job was safe and secure. However, when he heard of the sad state of his home, he was moved to move. He risked his secure position and issued a request to the king to go back to Jerusalem and make a difference. When he arrived in Jerusalem, he agonized about the situation, visualized new possibilities, and then organized the people. Nehemiah was a liberating headlight whose "mind's eye" saw new possibilities and gave the people something to look forward to and work toward. A spirit of revival liberated and empowered a devastated and defeated people to rise up and rebuild their community. It all began with a leader who had a headlight consciousness and a vision.

Our Lord and Liberator, Jesus the Christ, took a small group of men and women who were oppressed, marginalized, and disinherited and began a liberating and redemptive movement that resulted in his followers being referred to as ones who had "turned the world upside down." This all began with a leader who had a headlight consciousness and a vision. On one occasion Jesus beheld the sad state of the dispossessed masses and put his finger on the problem: they were "sheep without a shepherd." He then cast a vision of possibilities for his disciples: "the harvest is plentiful, but the laborers are few." The sheep without a shepherd were in a problematic state; however, as a visionary Jesus saw redemptive possibilities and potential. He referred to them as a "harvest" in need of laborers who would recognize what they could become.

It must be noted that in both models, the visionaries were not blind to the complex challenges, harsh realities, and context of oppression that caused people to feel "harassed and helpless, like sheep without a shepherd." The church must be conscious of the complicated and crippling conditions that paralyze our communities and oppress and repress people. Dr. Zan Wesley Holmes Jr. inspired St. Luke "Community" United Methodist Church in Dallas with his pastoral and prophetic vision. He reminds us "that among the vital signs in a congregation is not only that it have its ear attuned to the Word, but also that it have its ears attuned to the world. It is a tragedy that the closer some congregations think they are to Jesus, the further they are removed from the world."[1] Nehemiah agonized over what he saw when he beheld the wrecked walls and crumbling conditions in Jerusalem. Jesus was "moved with compassion" when he saw the crowd and the circumstances that contributed to their dysfunction—he was upset over what he saw and perceived. Christians who seek to have the "mind of Christ" should also seek to have the "eyes of Christ."

The "eyes of Christ" will cause us to agonize and be moved with compassion as we are attuned to the Word and the world. The eyes of Christ are not blind to the evolving sophistication, shrewdness, and subtly of America's unresolved issues related to race and racism. The eyes of Christ are horrified at the bullying mentality of militarism that presides over United States foreign policy in the name of a war on terror. The eyes of Christ do not turn away from and ignore the "big pink elephant" of sexual dysfunction (incest, abuse, and misogynistic videos) that is fracturing families and ruining lives in the African American community. The eyes of Christ are filled with tears when they behold the mistreatment of the "least of these," who are trapped in a vicious cycle of unemployment (or underemployment), inadequate health care, a failing education system, second-class services, and Third World conditions. The eyes of Christ are sensitive to and not judgmental of a hip-hop generation that has been exposed to the worst that life has to offer and was wounded in the process and now acts out their pain. The eyes of Christ flinch at the prison industrial complex (that is, twenty-first-century slavery)—the epidemic incarceration of African American men and their glaring absence from institutions of higher learning, the family table, PTA meetings, and corporate boardrooms. The eyes of Christ are pained by economic apartheid in corporate America. The eyes of Christ wince at the policies of greed, domination, and exploitation that allow 10 percent of the world's population to consume 80 percent of the world's resources. The eyes of Christ hurt when they behold the suffering of God's children in Africa because of the lingering effects of colonialism—continued economic exploitation by the former colonial powers and government corruption. The eyes of Christ are burdened and bothered by genocide in northeast Africa and the pitiful plight of children orphaned by HIV and AIDS in sub-Saharan Africa. The eyes of Christ glare with anger at the mistreatment of indigenous people, who have been shamefully all but annihilated and now are confined to substandard living on U.S. reservations and elsewhere.

Vision is not blind to the wreckage of the world, or how things are, but in light of and in spite of the situation, sees how things should be. Headlights provide vision because they work best in the dark. Nehemiah saw the conditions of ruin, but then he perceived new possibilities. Jesus saw the misery of the masses and their possibilities as a "harvest." Mary McLeod Bethune went to the state of Florida with a vision of educating descendants of Africa who had been victimized by slavery and the backlash of Jim Crow segregation. It all began with a vision. She only had a potbellied stove and less than two dollars. However, she eventually purchased what was a dump heap, and now Bethune-Cookman College stands as a testimony to a vision and a visionary. She testified, "When I walk through the campus with its stately palms and well-kept lawns, and think back to the dump-heap foundation, I rub my eyes and pinch myself. And I remember my childish visions in the cotton fields."[2] Vision takes note of the "dump-heap" circumstances but sees the invisible and works to bring about the impossible.

The local church must be led and spiritually fed by a pastor and leadership team with a headlight consciousness and vision of what should be. This vision is not limited to what the church should be, but what the community, nation, and world should look like and what the church will look like as an agent of liberation and transformation. This kind of vision is God-sized. A God-sized vision may begin locally, but a God-sized vision has an "uttermost parts of the world" consciousness.

Receiving the Revelation

In order to receive the unique and distinctive vision that God has for your ministry, it is vital to understand that God has been providentially setting you up. Your experiences, exposure, and education have been nurturing and positioning you to receive the revelation of the future that will give you a headlight consciousness. Accordingly, it is necessary to have a sense of your calling and what God wants to uniquely accomplish through you. Benjamin Elijah Mays, who mentored Martin Luther King, often said in his chapel messages at Morehouse College, "To be able to stand the troubles of life, one must have a sense of mission and the belief that God sent him or her into the world for a purpose, to do something unique and distinctive; and that if he does not do it, life will be worse off because it was not done." Having a sense of calling sets the stage for receiving the vision that God has tailor-made for you.

Moreover, the vision is received when we spend time with the Lord. Moses received his vision of liberation on the "back side of the desert" in his "creative encounter" with Yahweh. Nehemiah, upon learning of the wretched conditions in Jerusalem, entered into a season of fasting and praying in order to hear from God so that he could make a difference. Jesus fasted and prayed in the wilderness, clarifying the mission and vision of his liberating ministry. At Friendship-West Baptist Church in Dallas, Texas, God has given us a vision of "Becoming a Christian Community within the Community that will transform the Community." I had attended conference after conference trying to discover what kind of ministry our church was going to have. I had borrowed information from ministries I admired, and for a while the church was an ecclesiastical stew of what I had seen others doing. I even organized a "Dream Team" of members whom I charged with coming up with our church's vision under my direction. Finally, one of our wise deacons said, "Pastor Haynes, God has called you to shepherd this flock and evidently God has a vision that God wants to get to us, THROUGH YOU!" That was my "aha moment of awareness." I went into a season of prayer, fasting, meditation, and reflection. Over the next year I had a series of experiences that helped give birth to the vision that is ordering the steps of our ministry. The vision was received after I spent time with the Lord. We are now in the process of developing a sixty-acre community that will house and headquarter ministries of empowerment, transformation, and liberation. It will be a "Gospel Galleria," a one-stop shop where all of the needs we have—spiritual, economic, educational, recreational, and social—can be met while providing housing and addressing issues of health care. When God made and called you, God had in mind what you were to do and how you would eventually look; therefore it is imperative that you spend time with your Maker to find out what you are made for and will eventually look like.

Unveiling What Has Been Revealed

I have often wondered if there should be a cemetery of buried dreams and visions. Tombstones would indicate the vision, the birth date of the vision, and the death of the vision. It would be interesting to note if the vision was a victim of suicide or homicide. Some visions have never come to fruition because they were not cast properly or because, once they were cast, neglect or an unresponsive audience murdered the vision. Also, some visions have been victimized by a lack of follow-through. They have great starting power but lack staying power. When Nehemiah cast his vision and began to mobilize the people, an unwelcoming and hostile committee began to attack him. When our Lord and Liberator preached his inaugural message of mission and vision in the synagogue, he was attacked. When you cast a vision, vision haters organize for the demise of the vision. Furthermore, it is possible for you to get in the way of the vision that God has entrusted to you. This is done when the vision is not shared strategically and with sensitivity.

Vision casting is vitally important and must be strategic and intentional. Dr. Samuel DeWitt Proctor reminded us, "It is one thing to know the 'is-ness' of things, and even better to know the 'ought-ness,' but then comes the 'therefore' of things, where we go and how we get started."

Jesus provides us with an excellent model for unveiling what God has revealed to us. Jesus began by sharing his vision with a small group. The small group, known as the disciples of the Lord, were educated, enlightened, and equipped, and they eventually took ownership of the vision. This paradigm of Jesus recognizes the importance of nurturing vision carriers who will help to negotiate change.

Every church has persons of influence who should not be ignored when you are casting God's vision. Vision sharing takes time and requires education and equipping. One of the most inspiring experiences I have had as a pastor was when I shared the vision that God had given me with key leaders during a retreat. They embraced the big picture, and then, in a facilitated discussion, they "unpacked" the vision by taking ownership of their role in the vision, outlining a strategic plan, and creating what has become our vision statement. I have also taken the time to teach the theological and biblical foundations for our vision to our leadership team.

It became apparent to me that I needed to serve as a thermostat and create the theological climate at our church, teaching us who we are and in whom we believed so that we could understand what we were called to do. Dr. Jeremiah Wright Jr. has insightfully noted the influence of context on a church and its ministry. He has also pointed out that many Black churches have adopted an alien theology that may have toxic consequences for the church and the community. I was surprised to discover that Bull Connor was a Sunday school teacher in his church. Martin Luther King Jr. and Bull Connor did not have the same theology or worship the same God. If Dr. King had worshiped the same God as Bull Connor, Jim Crow segregation would be alive and flourishing. Black churches in too many instances have been nurtured on a theology that is adversarial to the emancipation and empowerment of African Americans. For example, a prosperity gospel has infected our churches with a dangerous classism (which is the result of a middle-class gospel of American individualism) and an infatuation with a capitalistic version of Christianity. With this in mind, we began a series of presentations to our church leaders on liberation and Black theology. This has helped to create a mind-set with which we major in ministry to the "least of these," and our sense of ministry is not limited to benevolent acts of charity but also includes pursuing justice.

Jesus enlightened and equipped his disciples to become vision carriers. These vision carriers were taught who God is, who they were, whom they were called to minister to, and where they were called to minister. Vision carriers help to create a vision-conscious church community, which in turn sets the stage for shaping a vision-driven ministry.

Negotiating Change and Making Room for the Vision

Martin Luther King Jr. is celebrated as the Dreamer. He was more than a dreamer, however; he was a visionary who drum-majored a liberation parade that challenged and changed the status quo. He was not killed for dreaming. He was assassinated because his vision prophetically spoke truth to a powerful status quo. A God-sized vision will always challenge the territorial custodians of what has been. Change is painful and must be nurtured and negotiated, or the vision or pastoral tenure will be assassinated!

As African people, we are relational. One of the ways to negotiate change is to recognize the value that we place on relationships and relating. A vision can be from God, but it must be worked out among people. People will rebel and reject vision and change if they do not trust the leadership. It is of the utmost importance that relationships are cultivated, especially with those who will be affected by the vision and who will be expected to help make the vision a reality. This will foster trust. Jesus mastered and modeled this principle. Not only did he spend time teaching the disciples and ministering to the masses, but he also spent special time with his inner circle of disciples who would later play key roles in the spreading of the gospel and carrying out the mission and vision that he had shared with them. Cultivating relationships will take time, but it is an invaluable investment. My mother often said to me that "people aren't impressed with nor do they care how much you know if they don't know how much you care." When you are attempting to cast a vision that will usher in change, cultivating relationships that manifest how much you care can create a climate of welcome for the vision.

One of the best ways to cultivate relationships is to create channels of communication. A lack of communication will open a Pandora's box of misperception and misunderstanding. Communication with key leaders and the leadership team that addresses moving from point A to point B and how it will affect them, while emancipating and empowering them to come up with solutions and address problems, engenders a sense of ownership of the vision.

Accordingly, a vision will receive a warm welcome if a climate is created that emphasizes the unique call of your particular church and the fact that those who are a part of your church's ministry must have been called by God to that ministry "for such a time (and vision) as this." A vision-driven church operates with a called consciousness that saturates the membership of the church. This called consciousness enlightens, educates, and equips every member who has a sense of calling to ministry with a vision for that ministry in the context of the corporate call and vision of the church.

Every member should be taught that they are ministers called to a specific ministry. When the writer to the Ephesians exhorted them to "lead a life worthy of the calling" (Eph. 4:1), he was not addressing those who were called to pastoral or even pulpit ministry. We have often limited "the call" to pulpit or pastoral ministry. Or we have limited the opportunities to serve in the church to standing as ushers, serving as deacons, singing in the choir, or working with youth and children. All of these are noble and necessary, but the complex challenges and insidious issues that confront our world in general and African people in particular call for an openness to persons to respond to God's call to use them to make a difference, even if what they do is not what we expect. This means that the church should make room for persons to discover and develop the call that the Lord has for their lives. This may result in the forming of new ministries that jump "out of the box" of our traditional concept of ministry. For example, there are a number of churches that provide ministry to abused and battered women and their children. These ministries have often been started by those who felt the call to this ministry facilitated by a climate of healing and freedom to explore what God wants that person to do, even if it were something new and untraditional. The myriad challenges and needs that afflict and affect the community and the world in which the church ministers provide numerous possibilities for ministries and opportunities for individuals to discover their particular calls and develop their particular visions. When members of the church sense and see themselves as ministers called to ministry, they take ownership of the vision.

It is also important that the church's vision emancipates and equips members (ministers) to refuse to limit their calling to ministry to the local church and community. Jesus called and commissioned us to go into the "uttermost parts of the world." The church should be a launching pad that empowers members to "take off" in ministry, even if it takes them "one step beyond." A vision-conscious church will also be a globally conscious church. Jeremiah Wright and Willie Wilson annually take their members on ministry tours and trips to the "uttermost parts of the world." This has heightened consciousness of the need for ministry internationally and expanded the horizons of people who discovered their call on a trip that took them beyond their own personal borders.

Finally, a vision-driven church must not limit its concept of ministry to the poor to charitable acts of benevolence, feeding the poor a fish, or even teaching them how to fish. Moses did not ask Pharaoh for handouts or even benefits and a salary. Moses confronted the injustice of slavery and told Pharaoh to let God's people go. Injustice continues to manifest itself in foreign policy that exploits Third World countries and in domestic policies that feed the prison industrial complex and create a climate for corporate apartheid and racist redlining. These are but a few examples of the injustices that must be confronted and changed. So the church must not limit its ministry to feeding a fish to the poor or even teaching them how to fish, but the church needs to ensure that the lake is free of contaminants and then empower the disadvantaged to buy the lake.

The persons who flock to our churches must have their consciousness raised by a conscious pulpit to be aware of the injustices anywhere that are "a threat to justice everywhere."[3] The voices of prophetic protest should be informed, inspired, and mobilized to make a difference strategically and with intentionality. Bishop Vashti Murphy McKenzie, while pastoring in Baltimore, and Dr. Willie Wilson in Washington, D.C., both organized churches in their communities to collectively challenge banks in their cities to respect and compete for the business of African Americans and the Black church. Churches joined forces and convinced the banks that it was good business to do business with the Black church and the African American community. These banks signed a covenant with the member churches, and it is well known which banks are friendly to African American interests in employment and community reinvestment.

Dr. King challenges us, even today, to be headlights, providing leadership, vision, and direction. One of our great headlight visionaries was the late, great Dr. Leon Howard Sullivan. He often shared the story of Hannibal, the North African freedom fighter and military genius. Hannibal brilliantly took thousands of soldiers and dozens of elephants to a showdown with Rome. He and his army came to the impossibly impassable Alps. He raised his hand, signaling to all behind him that they were to stop. He took his sword from his sheath and pointed it to the mighty mountains and shouted, "Behold the Alps." Each section of soldiers repeated the words of their visionary leader. After all of the soldiers had repeated him, he again pointed toward the overwhelming mountainous obstacle and shouted, "Behold the Alps." His followers repeated him again, but now they were feeling afraid. Then Hannibal raised his sword again and said, "Forward march. We see no Alps." Buoyed and energized by the courage of their visionary leader who not only saw the problematic obstacle but also envisioned their possibility, the soldiers followed him to their destiny. Every pastor must have the spirit of Hannibal and dare to shout, "Behold the Alps." There are problems that threaten to destroy our community. Behold the Alps. Injustice and racism deny our dignity and paralyze our progress. Behold the Alps. Internal issues like cancer are attempting to kill us from within. Behold the Alps. However, visionaries see and invite our members who are now ministers to seize our destiny. "Forward march. We see no Alps."

4.

Piety and Liberation

A Historical Exploration of African American Religion and Social Justice

Larry Murphy

THE RELIGIOUS IDENTITY OF AFRICAN AMERICANS is diverse and complex. It draws upon the heritage of their African past, the faith traditions encountered in their transplanted, diasporan home, and their own creative spiritual discernments. From these sources, over successive generations, they synthesized vital constructs of belief and practice as they sought to make meaning out of their existence.

A growing body of research evidence reveals that imported Africans retained significant aspects of their traditional religious life. Enslaved Muslims continued to practice their piety in prayer observances, in transcriptions of Qur'anic texts, and in observance of prescribed modes of dress and personal behavior. At the same time, Christian evangelistic efforts, organized and informal, sometimes even clandestine, led a significant number of enslaved and free Africans to the acceptance of Christianity. The enslaved worshiped in the churches of their owners and gathered in the informal meetings of the "Invisible Institution," the slave church. The legally free also met in congregations with whites and in the services of the emerging independent Black denominations.

Protestant Christianity in the United States, under whose influence most Blacks came, emphasized "experiential piety." It sought to foster a direct, personal encounter between the individual and the Holy God, an encounter that would be destabilizing, first, and then reconstructive of one's interior life—and, it was hoped, of one's daily walk. It was a momentous and effective encounter. For the enslaved or the socially proscribed free Black person, encountering God in Christian conversion was a radically liberating moment, addressing the very deepest levels of personhood. It brought Black people from the existential angst and social degradation of their condition to a state of transcendent affirmation and empowerment. Such an experience could not be contained; it had to be shared, in both the retelling of it and the invitation to others to a like encounter. And so one dimension of piety was a genuine sharing of the salvific "good news." Black clergy and laity extended to others the appeal to experience for themselves the transforming power of God. Blacks' personal evangelism was not race specific; they openly witnessed to whoever would receive the message (even if some may have had a special burden for Blacks since they tended to be underserved by existing religious bodies). Jarena Lee is a good nineteenth-century example of this evangelistic thrust. Her autobiography offers an amazing account of her travels—on foot, by coach, on river vessel—whatever would take her across the thousands of miles and several states she traversed as a bearer of the gospel to all classes and identities of people.[1]

As African Americans began to organize into independent congregations and larger associational bodies, the evangelistic impetus found expression early in initiatives for overseas missions. These initiatives were grounded in some enduring, impelling assumptions. One assumption, shared across the larger U.S. Christian community, was that salvation and regeneration, social uplift and advancement— often phrased as "progress and civilization"—were tied inseparably to Christianity, especially Protestant Christianity. The other assumption was that though separated by time and complex social-historical circumstances, there nevertheless was an intimate tie of spiritual and familial kinship between U.S. Blacks and Africans on the continent and in the diaspora. Hence, Black Christians in the United States engaged in early and continuous missional efforts to "redeem" Africa through Christian evangelism and through facilitating the social and economic development that went hand in hand with it.

The involvement of African American churches in missions is more fully understood when viewed in the context of their larger perceived *mission*, a tri-dimensional construct. The most obvious and ostensibly pursued mission of Black churches has been evangelism. This is an inheritance from the revivalistic Protestantism of the eighteenth and nineteenth centuries, upon which Black church life was largely modeled.

A second dimension of the African American church conception of its mission is the celebration of what is seen as the wondrous, saving works of God in history—personal histories and social history. Deliverance is both internal/spiritual and also external, in relationship to the concrete challenges and opportunities of the world. Thus, in lifting up God's interventions in history, some African Americans were led to the belief that justice-seeking and equity-seeking in this world are consonant with God's will. And so, the third dimension of the mission of the Black church has been human liberation, particularly focused on Black people, though not exclusive of any others.

A sense of mission understood in this manner is pervasive among Black congregations and denominations across the board. It is seen in the affirmation bestowed upon such persons as Martin Luther King Jr., Leon Sullivan, Willie Barrow, William Gray, and other Black clergy who have served as social advocates in the public forum, in industry, and in government. One should not expect that every or even most Black congregations are socially activist, only that most at some level will resonate positively with the notion of the church as a legitimate agent in the pursuit of the abundant life, the life of social righteousness and equity for all peoples. Further, while "the Black church" is used here as a convenient summary reference term, one must always bear in mind that the Black church is a heterogeneous entity with a composite identity. It spans virtually the full spectrum of ecclesiastical, theological, liturgical, socioeconomic, regional, and other particularities—this being so even within given denominational and confessional associations.

A retrospective look at aspects of Black religious thought and initiatives over the last two centuries will help to illuminate the diverse ways in which the Black church's tri-dimensional conception of mission has been articulated and actualized amid the challenges of African American life.

The Nineteenth Century

Running throughout the writings and public speeches of free Black clergy in the nineteenth century was an understanding of God's relationship to the world that provided the theological framework for the liberation thrust of free Black clergy. They understood that God was the Supreme Creator who established the principles by which the universe and all its constituent parts were to function, including the human community. As such, it was God who was the source of human rights; they were neither the result of humanity's largesse nor subject to its capricious manipulation. God as the guarantor of the order that God had created was thus also the vindicator of the oppressed. The language that free Blacks used to articulate this position drew from both the biblical text and the "rights of man" philosophical jargon of the Revolutionary War era. But the concepts were resident in Blacks' intuitive sense concerning the nature and inviolability of freedom itself. As such, the same sentiments are present in the recorded utterances of enslaved Blacks as well as the legally free.

Alongside this theological construct was the social analysis Blacks drew upon to explain their perennial, seemingly endemic condition as a socially proscribed people, exploited for their labor while excluded from the prerogatives of citizenship. It was not a simple analysis. It involved both a reading of the human makeup and a reading of the American mind. One aspect of the analysis attributed the abusive exploitation of Blacks directly to human self-interest and human sin. Those who engaged in oppression were evildoers, perverting justice and wantonly pursuing their own gain in ways that had always been part of the human enterprise. Another aspect of the analysis, one that Blacks found equally compelling, was that whites labored under misinformation and a misperception concerning the fundamental worth and social capacities of African Americans and their intentions relative to their role in American society. Partly because of this misinformation and misperception and partly because of human inadequacy, whites made a faulty application of the noble ideals, principles, and statutory provisions of the body politic. Blacks were aware of the inevitability of human sin and its pervasive consequences, which was their daily, lived reality. But they were also convinced of the capacity for the correctability of the American process, the prospect that white Americans could be brought around to do right by Blacks.

The interplay of the Black church's sense of mission with Blacks' theology and social analysis resulted in a variety of strategic responses to the Black condition, depending on the particular perspective on these three held by given clergy and laity.

One such response was to provide, through the priestly, devotional ministries of the church—whether the church among the free or the Invisible Institution of the enslaved—spiritual sanctuary, "shelter in the time of storm." Worship and devotional gatherings became spaces of hope and survival. In the presence of the Divine and in the company of those who shared one's lot, one could find sustenance and renewal, encouragement and strength to "fight another day," indeed to "run on to see what the end will be."

Another strategy involved building upon the assumptive good-will of the American people and the American political process. This could mean pursuing ordinary avenues of responsible personal and vocational living within established social structures and provisions. Demonstrating one's positive, productive, "regular" deportment would provide the counterdata to the white misperceptions concerning Blacks' fitness for social inclusion. More assertively, this strategy could mean employing moral suasion to change proscriptive laws and customs and to secure the institution of statutory and other measures for the inclusion of Blacks in the rights and prerogatives of citizenship. This included direct appeals to influential citizens, elected officials, and legislatures. For instance, in 1800 a group of Black Philadelphians under the leadership of the Reverend Absalom Jones submitted a petition to Congress seeking an end to the slave trade and the Fugitive Slave Act of 1793.[2] Others employed journalistic advocacy and persuasion, either through the majority press or through Black-established newspapers, as in Philip A. Bell's *Freedom's Journal*, edited by the Reverend Samuel B. Cornish, or the Reverend John J. Moore's paper *The Lunar Visitor*.

An even more broadly structured expression of the moral suasion strategy was the series of periodic, sometimes annual, state and national conventions organized among Blacks throughout the nineteenth century to discuss issues pressing upon the Black community and to devise effective methods of remedy. Clergy and active laity were prominent in leadership and participation in these conventions, which typically met in Black church buildings. The conventions often issued position papers directed to Black and white audiences, sponsored petition drives to influence legislation, and commissioned public speaking tours to inform and to generate initiatives toward amelioration of specific negative conditions. The inaugural National Negro Convention was held in 1831, called and presided over by the Right Reverend Richard Allen.

A third category of missional, strategic response to Black oppression was the initiation of alternative community service structures. The eighteenth century saw the emergence of Black Baptist, Methodist, and Episcopal congregations in several cities, including Silver Bluff, South Carolina, Lynchburg, Virginia, Baltimore, Philadelphia, Wilmington, Delaware, New York City, and Savannah. By the end of the nineteenth century, the numerical and organizational development of such movements toward independence had resulted in the formation of several predominantly Black denominations, including the seven Baptist, Methodist, and Pentecostal bodies often referred to as the "historically Black churches." The number has since continued to grow. These communions and their local congregations hosted or sponsored primary and secondary schools, collegiate institutions, and vocational training programs. Typically housed in the churches, the primary and secondary schools frequently had clergy as principals and teachers—who were typically the most educated and respected among community leaders—until public school boards could be persuaded to provide regular school facilities and staffing. Education was a high priority, as it was seen as the "lever of social elevation." The Reverend Prince Hall founded the Masonic order that still bears his name and that, with the women's Order of the Eastern Star, was received by the churches as a congenial partner in Black community service and character development. Local congregations were also the common venues for the organization of literary societies and similar cultural and educational groups, as well as mutual aid societies, whose function was to provide emergency relief for individuals or families experiencing crises because of illness, unemployment, natural disaster, or death. Given the obvious insurance character of these organizations, it is not surprising that many eventually transitioned from this church base into actual insurance and financial service companies.

Other strategies of social intervention involving clergy and churches took sometimes more, sometimes less assertive expressions, or some combination of these, depending on the circumstances and the perspective of the leadership.

Richard Allen, former slave and highly respected leader in the late eighteenth and early nineteenth centuries, was a pivotal figure in the independent Black church movement—in large measure a protest against discrimination in church life. He also played a leading role in a boycott against slave-made commercial goods. Yet Allen's primary approach to Black oppression might be characterized as moral appeal: he appealed to the consciences and to the sense of self-interest of both whites and Blacks to live up to their Christian duty. If this were done, he argued, whites would end their oppression, and Blacks would maintain a positive standing before God.

It appears that in Allen's view—observed in many of his sermons to white audiences and Black audiences, God would not condone the violation of the demands of piety, even for the sake of liberation from loathsome bondage. Having come out of slavery himself, surely Allen was torn by the image of other Blacks still laboring in chains. As a person of faith and human sensitivity, he must have been wrestling with the question of what it meant to be a Christian and a slave. This same tension was evidenced in the case of Josiah Henson, who balked at slaying four sailors who were carrying him to reenslavement in the Deep South, even though the act might have assured his safe escape. Allen, Henson, and others of their orientation understood nonviolent moral appeal to be the liberation strategy that was most consistent with the dictates of piety. At the same time, Allen was a leader in what was intended to be a widespread boycott of consumer goods produced by the enslaved. Thus, while there was to be no assault on persons, both moral and financial pressure could be brought to bear on systems.

The Reverend Prince Hall, like Allen, dedicated his energies to the betterment of life for Black people. He established a school for Black children and was the founder of the first Black Masonic order in the United States. Hall sympathized with liberation efforts that went beyond appealing to whites, petitioning Congress, or even boycotts. He spoke with encouragement about the successful Black revolution in Haiti. He saw in the victory of that effort the hope that Blacks in the United States could achieve freedom if they worked together. Hall did not openly advocate violent strategies; his own activities were within established legal boundaries. But seemingly he was not averse to subversive or even armed resistance, should it come to that. Similar in approach to Hall was the Reverend Jeremiah Burke Sanderson, an abolitionist orator in the East. Later, on the west coast he was a noted educator in Black public schools and was among those who became adept at spiriting away Blacks who were illegally held in slavery.

The Reverend Henry Highland Garnett combined orthodox piety and aggressive Black resistance. In a speech before the 1843 meeting of the National Negro Convention, Garnett's message to the enslaved stated:

> In every man's mind the good seeds of liberty are planted, and he who brings his fellow down so low as to make him contented with a condition of slavery, commits the highest crime against God and man. . . . To such degradation it is sinful in the extreme for you to make voluntary submission. The divine commandments you are in duty bound to reverence and obey. . . . You are not certain of heaven, because you suffer yourselves to remain in a state of slavery, where you cannot obey the sovereign of the universe.

If willful acquiescence in a system that inhibited the performance of one's Christian duties was a source of culpability for Blacks, the remedy was clear: "The diabolical injustice by which your liberties are cloven down, neither God, nor angels, nor just men, command you to suffer for a single moment. Therefore it is your solemn and imperative duty to use every means, both [*sic*] moral, intellectual, and physical that promises success."

Whereas Richard Allen saw patience in the unmerited suffering of slavery as a prelude to eternal reward, Garnett saw it as a sin leading to hell. Whereas Allen rejected violent resistance as contrary to piety, and Prince Hall only sympathized with it, Garnett advocated it as a fully acceptable option within Christian duty. Indeed, he heralded insurrectionists Denmark Vesey and Nat Turner (also a Baptist preacher) as "noble and brave" and claimed that Joseph Cinque accomplished his revolt aboard the slave ship *Amistad* "by the help of God." And while Garnett called upon the enslaved to revolt, the Reverend Moses Dickson organized in 1856 the Knights of Tabor, or Knights of Liberty, a large (forty-seven thousand) secret volunteer army whose purpose was to fight for the emancipation of the enslaved. Drawing their name from the biblical narrative in which Israel successfully did battle for its freedom, they were confident that God would support them in their cause. According to Dickson, only the eruption of the Civil War prevented and made unnecessary the prosecution of their well-laid plans.[3]

If Black churches and their clergy did not have widespread involvement in such initiatives for the physical overthrow of slavery, several did join in the clandestine insurgency of the Underground Railroad. Many today can still point with pride to the passageways and holding rooms in their church buildings where "passengers" were secreted away at these stations on their journey to the North and to Canada.

The Reverend John James Moore and the Reverend Dr. Edward Wilmot Blyden were of that minority contingent of Northern Black leaders who advanced emigration as the solution to the Black social dilemma. Doubtful that white America would ever do right by people of color, emigrationists argued that it would be better for Blacks to remove to some fertile, potentially prosperous location outside of the United States where they could establish a model nation for themselves, or at least find better opportunities for social and economic elevation. Moore, who served an African Methodist Episcopal (AME) Zion church in San Francisco, joined with a party of some hundreds of Blacks, who departed the country in 1858 and settled in British Columbia. Blyden, who in 1850 came from the Virgin Islands to study in the United States, was struck by the biblical statement that

"Ethiopia shall soon stretch out her hands unto God" (Ps. 68:31), which he, as did some other Christians, interpreted to mean that Africa would one day emerge as a great world power. Placing this in the context of his Presbyterian theology, Blyden believed that Blacks' importation to the United States was providentially ordained as a means of exposure to Western technology and the Christian religion. Black Americans were duty-bound to take these resources back to Africa so that, in concert with resident African culture, which Blyden fully affirmed, the continent could be redeemed and empowered and the biblical prophecy fulfilled. Failing to elicit any significant numerical response to his plea for Black emigration to Africa, Blyden himself settled in West Africa and was active in political and intellectual life there until his death in 1912.

In the post–Civil War, late-nineteenth-century period, African Americans' assessment of the root causes of the challenges facing them remained essentially the same. So too did their basic response strategies, although their ostensibly changed circumstances, most notably the end of legal slavery, buoyed their hopes that things could be different. Black state and national conventions and local activist groups devised initiatives for taking advantage of the rights and protections now legally extended through the enactment of the Thirteenth, Fourteenth, and Fifteenth Amendments to the Constitution. They pressed local school boards to actualize the statutorily mandated public school provisions for Blacks; they organized voter information and registration campaigns and even fielded candidates for public office (including some clergy). Clergy and laity continued to be active in these efforts. Furthermore, the churches extended themselves in energetic ways to embrace and minister to the newly freed. The combination of an active, focused evangelistic effort on the part of Northern Black churches with an eager disposition on the part of the newly freed to affiliate with Black institutions resulted in Black church membership quadrupling in size in the decades following the end of the Civil War. More than ever before, Black churches became the focal public institutions in their communities, the coalescing points for educational and cultural enrichment, community building, and character development. The churches helped their communities navigate the social and political forces that still impinged upon Black life, albeit in new forms now that slavery had segued into the opportunities of "freedom," marred by the upsurge of Jim Crow discrimination. Of course, the churches continued their pastoral and priestly ministries of spiritual, existential sustainment through the passages of life.

The Twentieth Century: The Early Decades

Following the Civil War and the successive state-by-state failure of Reconstruction, the newly freed African American population took up the notion of leaving the South. In 1879 the Reverend Benjamin "Pap" Singleton was involved in a movement of some fifty thousand African Americans from southern Louisiana towns to resettle in the state of Kansas. It was a move to counter the harsh social conditions and prevalent anti-Black violence, as well as the bleak economic prospects of Blacks living in the post–Civil War, post-Reconstruction South.

What had been progressing sporadically and on a small scale became, at the turn of the twentieth century, a pivotal event in the life of African Americans, and indeed the nation as a whole, with the massive Black demographic shift known as the "Great Migration." Continuing poor economic conditions in the South, a persistent, vicious Jim Crow environment, combined with new and promising employment opportunities in the North led to what became the largest internal migration the country had ever experienced. Beginning in 1910 and taking on flood-tide force in 1916, millions of African Americans eventually left their traditional rural Southern homeland for the cities of the South and especially the North, or the "promised land." Often in the forefront of these relocation initiatives was a local pastor, who might encourage the congregation to accept the appeal of Northern labor recruiters or, invited to a Northern city to preach a revival and seeing firsthand the positive prospects, might invite the congregation to reconstitute itself in the new, Northern venue. Sometimes congregation members who had already migrated North would appeal to their pastor to move North to be their leader.

As Black churches became established in the cities, their clergy leaders came to represent significant potential social and political power and were advancing multifaceted social ministries. Chicago is a representative case. The city's Quinn Chapel AME Church thrived under such pastors as the Reverend Archibald J. Carey Jr., who was also a judge, a business owner, an adviser to a U.S. president, and a prominent member of Chicago political circles. Carey worked to extend employment opportunities for African Americans, and he was responsible for the first public park to be located in Chicago's Black community. At Olivet Baptist Church, Pastor L. K. Williams initiated such programs as a kindergarten, a day nursery, a health bureau and free clinic, classes in nutrition and home health care (staffed by Red Cross nurses), a branch of the Chicago Public Library, a Working Girls' Home, and a schedule of movies, offered for education and entertainment. A statement contained in the church's 1922 anniversary souvenir book asserted that "uplifting and serving a community is the essential, reasonable counterpart of acceptable divine service."[4] The institutional AME had an employment bureau, a print shop, a kindergarten, a gym, and classes in cooking, sewing, and music. Pilgrim Baptist had a cooperative buying club; Fulton Methodist sponsored a Health Education Council. These congregations, along with many others, offered social programs and support services that in some cases kept their facilities open twenty-four hours a day. And beyond the church proper, evangelist Amanda Berry Smith operated her Industrial School for Girls.

As the twentieth century progressed, African Americans increased incrementally but steadily their involvement in business, the professions, and politics, producing additional, in some cases alternative, centers of social authority and leadership. But if the churches did not remain in the absolute, exclusive leadership posture, the churches and their clergy continued their immense importance as the strongest, wealthiest corporate presence in the Black community. Indeed, churches and clergy were expected to concern themselves with advancing Black interests and well-being. The clergy were to be "Race Men," for even in the promising environment of the Northern city, challenges to Black well-being and socioeconomic advancement were discovered to be formidable.

Not all or even most congregations carried memberships and budgets that would enable broad social ministries. There were many congregations of the "storefront" type—occupying small, available commercial spaces on the way to affording regular church-type facilities. These congregations, especially Pentecostal or holiness churches, were intimate, personally affirming, and cathartic, while at the same time rigorous and strict in expectations of personal behavior. They combated the disintegrating forces of urban life and provided avenues for personal empowerment. While one may have been socially dispossessed and poor, one could be "saved, sanctified, and filled with the Holy Ghost," rich in status before God and armor-clad against the darts of devils—spiritual or human. Storefront churches were important sanctuary spaces and mutual learning centers as migrants learned how successfully to negotiate their security amid the rough currents of city living.

For some, though, neither the more established congregations of the historic Black churches nor the storefronts were sufficient to address the hurting points of Black life. They turned to innovative religious alternatives. In the midst of a fiercely segregated society,

Father Divine's Peace Mission "heavens," as he called them, were places where Blacks and whites could interact on terms of perfect equality. There, in the material uncertainty of Depression days, one partook in a lifestyle that previewed the harmony and abundance of the New Age. Then there were those groups that took on the issue of identity, a major internal struggle for a people variously defined in society as three-fifths of a person, as non-person, as human degenerates, as cultureless pariahs. William Christian told Blacks that they were of the same race—the Black race—as the biblical Abraham, David, and Jesus. Others, such as Prophet Cherry, took this honored identification with scriptural personages a further step to assert that African Americans were actually Jews, or the "real" Jews, the lost tribes of Israel, or some similar affiliation. Using a parallel approach but a different identity, some groups cast African Americans as Moors or Middle Eastern "Asiatics," whose correct and proper religion was Islam. There was the Moorish Science movement of Timothy Drew, also known as Noble Drew Aliand the Original Tents of Kedar, under the leadership of As Sayyid Al Imaam Issa Haadi Al Mahdi (H). Perhaps the most familiar of such groups is the one established by Elijah Poole, later Elijah Muhammad, and known today as the Nation of Islam. In these various forms of identity movements, with their currents of nationalism, piety addressed liberation through an existential self-naming, a self-definition of a cultural group within the society on terms that replaced societal degradation with a valorization of the people grounded in a transcendent realm. It addressed issues of racial and cultural integrity and self-esteem through an asserted revelation of African Americans' "true," valuable selves.[5]

Mid-Century and Beyond

African American Christian piety was a core element in the mid-century emergence of the Civil Rights Movement. With committed lay and clergy leadership such as Rosa Parks, Fannie Lou Hamer, Andrew Young, Martin Luther King Jr., Ralph Abernathy, Wyatt Walker, Joseph Lowery, and Prathia Hall, among many others, statutory racial discrimination and its counterparts in general social practices were challenged and largely transformed. Churches were the venues for organizing and the source for much of the human power for the marches, demonstrations, boycotts, and other components of the movement's strategy of nonviolent resistance. The Reverend Leon Sullivan's Opportunities Industrialization Centers, Rev. Jesse Jackson's Operation PUSH (People United to Save/Serve Humanity), and other initiatives focused on what many determined was a core element in any drive toward African American social empowerment, namely, economic empowerment and equity in employment and the consumer marketplace. In previous decades, A. Phillip Randolph and the Reverend Adam Clayton Powell, among others, developed similar strategies and initiatives. Here at mid-century the movement came together and garnered mass participation from Blacks and whites and from various racial and religious communities.

The segue from the social centrality of the Civil Rights Movement to the more assertive days of the late 1960s and 1970s provided a unique context for African American Christians' feelings concerning piety and liberation. Many who were comfortable with the movement's boycotts and sit-ins, and even its other acts of civil disobedience, were not as embracing of what they saw as the "militancy" of appeals to "Black Power." On the one hand, asserting Black identity was received as a call to affirm what had become stigmatized and degraded in the general culture, as well as among African Americans themselves. Whether casually "playing the dozens" (joking, ribbing, "dissing") or engaging in serious, hostile verbal repartee, to call someone "Black" was the ultimate insult. On the other hand, to assert an identity separate from one's Americanness was to contradict what had been the explicit and implicit thrust of generations of Civil Rights and social justice activism, a denial of the motivating goal of social acceptance and inclusion. Further, asserting power was suggestive of employing physical force and raised both the long-standing issue of the security of Blacks' being in a confrontation with overwhelming white power and the question of the legitimacy of Christians' use of physical force for social aims. In the nineteenth century Garnett had urged the enslaved to "strike for your lives and liberties,"[6] preacher Nat Turner led an armed revolt, and the Reverend T. M. D. Ward (later an AME bishop) spoke of the Union armies in the Civil War as God's arm of deliverance. Even Richard Allen had pointed to the conquering Cyrus of Hebrew scriptures as an instrument of God. Yet African American Christian piety had always contained an alternative strand that eschewed violence, counseled forbearance in oppression, and relegated the initiation of force for justice's sake to God.

If African American Christians as a whole did not embrace Black Power as physical militancy, some segments of the church seized upon other avenues for the assertion of power in affirming the integrity of Black identity. Student and faculty agitation in the 1960s and 1970s led to the establishment of courses and later whole departments focusing on teaching and research relative to the social and historical development of peoples of African descent. African American religious studies was a natural, essential part of this developing domain. James Cone's publication in 1969 of his seminal work *Black Theology and Black Power* spurred a proliferation in religion departments and theological schools of courses and publications on the religious thought and practices of Black peoples, including the development of effective courses for training clergy and lay leaders for Black congregations. The year 1970 saw the formation of the Society for the Study of Black Religion, an organization of professors and researchers whose purpose was to engage in scholarly research and discussion of the religious experience of Blacks in order to enrich their and others' work and to encourage the incorporation of Black religious studies into the curricula of colleges, universities, and seminaries.

Critical, reflective thought honoring the integrity of the Black religious experience took a variety of forms. The Black Theology Movement probed the authoritative source materials of Christian faith, including scripture, doctrinal traditions, and Black experience itself, to discern the kerygmatic message for the oppressed, for those, in theologian Howard Thurman's words, whose "backs were against the wall." It inspired similar efforts at liberative theological reflection among other socially beleaguered groups, both in the United States and abroad. A corollary development emerged among some Black female theologians who sought to extend Black theological analysis to account for gender dynamics and recognition that Black women suffer under the triple oppression of sex, race, and class. This complementary womanist theology, like Black theology, from which it emerged, has found a significant place in the theological academy. Mutually supportive with these developments are Black biblical hermeneutics and critical Black scholarly work in historical studies, theological ethics, religious sociology, homiletics, Christian education, psychology and personality, and church administration. There have been longitudinal projects such as the Black Theology Project and research and strategy centers such as the Leadership Center at Morehouse College in Atlanta.

All of these developments and initiatives, along with the hundreds, perhaps thousands, of books, essays, and conference presentations that have come about over the last several decades, aim to illuminate for African Americans the nexus of intentional thought about God, devotional piety that responds to the divine–human encounter, and the living out of the implications of Christian faith amid the relationships and concrete challenges and opportunities of life in community.

Further, one discovers that the interface of African American Christian churches within the branches of the Christian family takes on this same character of conjoining piety and liberation. For while Black denominations have long been active participants in the ecumenical movement, with Black clergy even serving terms as administrative heads of national and international interfaith organizations, among Black denominations ecumenism has not focused on issues of doctrine, polity, or organizational unity. Instead, Black ecumenism has centered on interdenominational cooperation in addressing issues of community development, social justice, and liberation. That was the case with the formation of the Fraternal Council of Negro Churches in the 1930s. It continues so today with the Congress of National Black Churches (CNBC), a consortium of eight historically Black denominations that, according to its newsletter, is "built on the premise that despite doctrinal differences, our common goals would hold us together." CNBC is dedicated to amicable relationships among the member denominations while working "toward the common good of people of African descent" and from the desire "to see all of God's children free." Since its founding in the late 1970s, CNBC has fostered programs in justice and public safety (for example, its National Anti-Drug/Anti-Violence Campaign and its HIV/AIDS Awareness Program), voter registration and education, community and economic development, leadership development, enhancement of access to information technology, environmental justice, and health care, among others.[7]

The Contemporary Church

Piety and liberation continue as two explicit dimensions of the African American churches. To be sure, the decline in membership and participation that has challenged most U.S. denominations over the last three decades has not given Black churches a "bye." Evidence for this is the intense concern about strategies for evangelism and church growth expressed everywhere in the church, from local congregational meetings to national judicatory conventions and conferences to the spate of publications and workshops offering guidance for congregational expansion. At the same time, this period has seen two other developments. One is a neo-Pentecostal liturgical renewal that has transcended denominational lines with exuberant, expressive worship behaviors once associated only with the smaller, even marginalized holiness and Pentecostal communions. Indeed, the Church of God in Christ (COGIC), the more prominent among these churches, has become one of the largest historically Black denominations. And once genuinely devotional but behaviorally reserved congregations are "raising holy hands," "giving God a hand clap of praise," and reverberating to music on which one can "cut a step" (some clergy and laity actually doing so) and are deeply engaged in prayer, fasting, and studying the Word. The second development is the emergence of "mega-churches," congregations that exceed ten thousand members and occupy huge campuses of worship and learning/serving spaces. These too tend to be energized by a lively worship mode and expository preaching that illumines and applies the scripture toward personal transformation and successful living.

Alongside this, though, Black churches, at the local and judicatory levels, continue to address issues of human need and social equity. In the 1970s and 1980s, Black congregations were adding "educational wings" to their buildings, responding to a renewed focus on social relevance and community service. But even tiny, "facilities-challenged" storefront churches offer meal service and clothing banks for the homeless. Congregations of all sizes and descriptions are active. The Appleton (Wisconsin) Sanctuary Outreach Ministries church has Bible study for the homebound, marriage workshops, a child abuse prevention program, a prayerful nutrition and Tae Bo exercise support group, and a stepping ensemble for youth that develops discipline and promotes self-esteem. The Mendenhall Church in Missouri sponsors a not-for-profit corporation that offers legal services, educational mentoring, and skills development. Liberty Baptist in Chicago cosponsors Vision House, a residence and support services center for families affected by HIV/AIDS. Bethel AME in Baltimore offers ministries for college students, substance abusers, people with cancer, the incarcerated, senior citizens, and couples, to name a few. The variety of ministries is myriad. Some are underwritten by the individual congregations; others are done in partnership with public and private agencies.

Piety and Liberation in African American Christianity: An Assessment

As stated above, African Americans did not inherit from social philosophy or from Christianity the urge for freedom; it did not take Revolutionary War rhetoric or liberation theology to confirm in them their legitimate right to an existence without arbitrary, abusive restriction. These are natural components of the human makeup. Thus, it would seem that protest and assertion of autonomy would be givens; they could be anticipated. And the record among Blacks of innumerable acts of personal social defiance and corporate insurrection would seem to bear this point out.

At the same time, there have been forces within African American life that supported quietism. There is a natural tendency in persons to seek stasis, a normal, predictable, manageable mode of daily living on a middle course between anxious insecurity and the focused, adrenalin-intensity of a movement. Further, there is a realism that assesses what seem to be the reasonable available options and opportunities, balanced against risks and dangers, and finally settling upon a course of sustainable existence. Still further, the circumstances of African American life often lead to a sense of alienation from society, as expressed (for example) in many songs. Nevertheless, Blacks desire to be at home in the world community and tend to seek acceptability in society by acting in conformity to its norms and values, demonstrating loyalty to and support of the social system. After all, it is a system that—in its positive aspects—African Americans had helped to create and defend against external foes.

There is a tendency to see piety and liberative action as polar ends of a submission-aggression continuum. That is a misreading. Piety was not one thing and liberation its antithesis. Rather, the latter often derived its motive power and its transcendent validation from the former. And equally pious clergy and laity could be found opting for differing points along the submission-aggression continuum, sometimes drawing from disparate points at the same time, in crafting a liberative strategy. While a given person's theology may have disqualified certain forms of action or privileged others, the fundamental, guiding issues were, "What makes sense as a strategy, given prevailing realities?" and "How do we live between God's will for our liberation and the demands inherent in what it means to be 'new creatures in Christ,' pursuing a higher vision of human relationship in community?"

The seminal study of African American religious life conducted by the late Dr. C. Eric Lincoln and his associate Dr. Lawrence Mamiya[8] phrases the issues in terms of dialectical tensions between polar values. The tensions most pertinent for our discussion are "otherworldly versus this-worldly," the "communal versus the privatistic," and "resistance versus accommodation." These point, on the one hand, to the pull to focus one's piety on accepting one's attributed place in society while enhancing one's spiritual life in preparation for the place of honor in the next life. On the other hand, they point to a focus on a self-affirming, active involvement in the present world, owning responsibility for the total well-being of members of the community, including political, economic, educational, social, cultural, and other aspects of their lives. As mentioned before, both of these vectors of piety have been operative in the traditions of the Black churches. We see the tension between these two orientations institutionalized in the creation of a new denomination. In 1960 forces within the National Baptist Convention, USA, clashed over the direction the Convention should take relative to social justice action on behalf of African Americans. The more accommodating camp, headed by the late Reverend Joseph H. Jackson, Convention president, managed to sustain its convention leadership. The challengers, Martin Luther King Jr. and Gardner Taylor among them, withdrew to form the new Progressive National Baptist Convention.

In 1967 Gary T. Marx published an article, "Religion: Opiate or Inspiration of Civil Rights Militancy among Negroes?" based on a study that gathered statistical data from interviews on religion and militancy, factoring in such variables as age, gender, education, geographic region of residence, and so forth. Marx concluded that "the greater the religious involvement . . . the lower the degree of militancy." Yet there are qualifiers: the *orientation* of one's religion makes a significant difference. For those whose focus is on the next life and those who believe that significant change must come at God's initiative, religion's effect is to inhibit protest and activism. Marx cites literature that suggests religion may become a substitute for social activism. For those with a temporal focus and/or a sense of the ability of humans (either alone or in concert with God) to achieve change, religion may support protest.[9]

Perhaps the matter of piety and liberation among African American Christians can be summed up in this way. The collective body of African American Christians, across the various lines of diversity, has borne deep concern over the issues and challenges facing Blacks and other peoples of color in the United States. Their churches have been sources of funding and of human resources for movements of social intervention. They have opened their facilities to serve the various purposes and needs of social justice movements, as well as social betterment causes of all types. Some even have standing organizational units (commissions, auxiliaries, clubs, and so forth) nominally dedicated to these purposes. Yet, the week-by-week focus of African American churches locally and at the judicatory levels has been on religious nurture and evangelism, understood as the saving of souls and the increase in the membership of the body of believers, along with maintenance of the institutional structures. What might be named as a liberationist or prophetic thrust, while always present as a subtext, does not often emerge as explicit institutional position statements, nor as sustained public institutionally sponsored action. The genuine, pervasive concerns for the amelioration of besetting social conditions more typically find their expression in public initiatives taken by individual clergy and laity, acting out of their own theological and social vision. They may have the tacit support of congregants and of denominational leadership, particularly if their involvement is not at the expense of fulfilling congregants' expectations regarding worship leadership, pastoral care, and institutional administration. On the other hand, some clergy and laity do not believe that it is appropriate for clergy to be involved in social advocacy. Their concept of the clerical task is centered on preaching and evangelism, though they may laud the pastor's leadership in establishing in-house programs of social service and charity.

Except for periods of intense racial hostility and assault, there is a broad accommodation among church members to the given social circumstances, so that the expectation placed upon pastors is that they simply will provide nurturing, caring, inspiring religious ministry through the endemic passages and changes, triumphs, defeats, and mundane rounds of existence and that the pastor will be a resource for meaning making in their lives, ennobling their struggles by locating them in a divine schema, supplanting existential anxiety with a ground of present security and future hope.

If a pastor, then, has a more encompassing theological vision that connects this kind of personal redemption with a faith-based call to social responsibility, s/he faces the challenge of nurturing congregants into that vision. Otherwise, they will see his/her activism as adjunct to, if not in competition with, the central pastoral task.

The Road Ahead

Lincoln and Mamiya concluded their volume on the Black church with a series of "Policy Recommendations for the Black Church." Their first and priority recommendation was for a better-educated, better-trained clergy, for this reason:

> Our survey and field experiences indicate quite clearly that the most innovative forms of ministry in Black communities today are being carried out by the better-educated clergy at the large urban Black churches. However, even if size were held constant, the better-educated clergy tend to be more resourceful in serving

smaller urban churches or even rural ones. They are also more aware of both the internal needs of their congregations, as well as the external needs in their surrounding communities.[10]

Other recommendations included improved benefits for clergy (for example, health care and pension); addressing the coming shortage of clergy to fill existing pulpits, partly by opening the channels for the full participation of women in the clerical ranks; and finding ways to enhance the cultural identity and self-esteem of Black youth as one lever of elevation out of the social and economic marginalization that characterizes much of the Black community, while correlatively moving Black youth toward personal accomplishment and social achievement.[11]

These recommendations look to the strengthening of the Black church and clearly grow out of the authors' conception of the Black church as a composite institution with a historic tradition and future mandate to be in holistic service to the Black community.

Similarly, pastor and university educator James Henry Harris writes that "mis-education, poor self-esteem and the failure of Black Christians to understand and appreciate their own history and culture is a real problem in Black churches. . . . Black folk . . . expect the pastor to help them cope with joblessness, poverty and discrimination by transforming their despair into hope. Black theology needs to provide the content and method for changing the social, economic and political obstacles for Blacks."[12]

Harris, like Lincoln and Mamiya, calls for recognizing women's leadership gifts and giving them equal access to ministerial orders. He calls on the Black church to address Black poverty by using its influence to affect public policy decisions related to affordable housing and employment opportunities.

Further, Harris presses Black churches in other areas: to become actively involved in local education by monitoring their constituents' progress through school, by coordinating efforts with teachers and counselors, and by providing mentoring assistance with schoolwork; to deploy church financial resources to invest in the Black community and thereby encourage other institutions to do likewise, thus strengthening the Black community as a viable living context; and to do a community needs assessment to inform and guide the congregation's planning of its ministry agenda.[13]

These two mandating visions for the Black church offered in the closing decade of the twentieth century are consonant with the assertion of nationally known pastor W. Franklyn Richardson on the eve of the new millennium: "Our fundamental message of healing and hope for African Americans is as significant as ever, but we need to connect it to the issues that most affect our community and will affect us in the future."[14]

Whether a prophetic engagement of the social order in pursuit of the equitable inclusion of African Americans in the rights and privileges, benefits and opportunities of U.S. society shall become the pervasive characterization of African American Christian churches, balancing their rich parallel tradition of vital, sustaining spiritual nurture, remains to be seen. Whether it is realistic to expect a parity relationship between piety and liberation in the missional vision of every congregation, or most congregations, existing as their members do amid the multiple pushes and pulls of personal passages and institutional challenges, is open for reflection. It is clear, though, that as much as at any other time, this moment calls for those who claim their baptism and seek to live out its implications to continue to seek that balance of the priestly, pastoral, and prophetic, the care of souls and the transformation of "this world of woe" into "the beloved community," wherein all may be participants in the "abundant life" that the faith tradition proclaims is the gift and the promise of God.

II

The Theological Imagination

5.

Loving God with Our Heart, Soul, and Mind

James H. Cone

PROFOUND SOUL-SEARCHING and vigorous intellectual reflection are necessary if we are to continue to grow in an understanding of our faith and of our calling. Reflecting on one's primary task in ministry is vital, not only at the beginning of one's ministry, but also throughout the course of that ministry.

As professor of Systematic Theology at Union Theological Seminary in New York, I have had many long discussions and debates about the importance of the teaching ministry with seminary students focused on pastoring. I suggest that these intellectually gifted students consider teaching because the Black church does not suffer for a lack of ministers who can proclaim the Word in the name of the Lord.

I am often amazed at the improvisational skills of the Black preacher who can speak about the power of God in such a way that one can feel the presence of the spirit in the midst of the congregation, empowering people with songs and words. After six days of coping with the great contradictions of life, Black people come to church on Sunday to hear a word from the Lord—a liberating word that heals broken hearts and troubled minds. They do not want to hear a dry, academic lecture. There is no substitute for the comforting and prophetic words that preachers provide for Black people who have been struggling against white supremacy for nearly four centuries.

No Black Christian can escape the agony of the question: Why did God make Blacks outcasts and strangers in their own home? Every Sunday and often throughout the week, pastors search for interesting and imaginative ways to reassure Black people that our God is able to make a way out of no way. God is able to give us the inner strength and resources in order to confront the trials and difficulties of this life. This is all that religion can guarantee. In fact, ministers should never say to our people that if you have faith in God, you will not have problems or misfortunes. We can say, however, if you have an authentic faith in God, God will give you that something within that will help you to stand up in the midst of personal and social trials and tribulations.

Ministers are both priest and prophet. They care for the souls who are wounded by personal loss and hurt, and they fight for justice for the people who have been wronged in society. The Black community has survived both spiritually and physically because we have had prophetic ministers who have stood before courageous crowds facing a hostile government in order to proclaim: let justice roll down like waters and righteousness as the mighty stream.

Therefore, my reason for advising students to consider theology as a vocation has nothing to do with my lack of regard for the importance of preaching. I have consistently reminded students that Jesus was not only a preacher but also a teacher. The teaching ministry is of equal importance to pastoral ministry. Unfortunately, the Black church is not known for promoting the intellectual side of the Christian ministry. We love God with our hearts and souls, but we often forget that we were also called to love God with our minds. The Black church suffers from a lack of intellectually accomplished and spiritually committed scholars who feel as deeply the need to understand the faith as preachers do to proclaim it.

Ministers need to think as well as pray. Without the right knowledge, white theology easily becomes the paradigm for Black preachers. If the Black church is not careful, it will become a church with a borrowed theology that is used to tame rather than liberate. It is the Black church's responsibility to do its own thinking about the gospel and not to depend on what white theologians say. If the Black church is going to deal creatively with the relevant issues of our time, develop transformative paradigms, implement effective strategies, then we have the responsibility to develop creative theology that will hold us accountable to the gospel of Jesus Christ. The Black church needs prophetic and professional theologians that help the preachers to understand the gospel and how to make it relevant in the twenty-first century.

We need to nurture a critical and prophetic theology to effectively minister to our congregations. We can develop great rhetorical skills, create effective programs of stewardship, discover ingenious schemes for church growth and management, and find creative ways to mobilize and fight for justice in society. But if we don't have a clear understanding of what the gospel means, we are lost and all the other things we do are meaningless. We cannot stay on the right track without a critical and prophetic theology as an essential guide. That was true of Martin Luther in the sixteenth century and of his namesake, Martin Luther King Jr., in the twentieth century.

Theology is not an option for the Black church. Theology is an indispensable tool for an understanding of Christian identity today. Unfortunately, too few Black people have developed the intellectual interest and passion to become first-rate scholars and theologians.

When I spot gifted students, an intellectual light turns on, and I seek to open the exciting world of theology to them, though some resist my pushing and shoving and choose to go into the pastoral ministry instead. They also usually assure me that they will not abandon the life of the mind, and most have remained true to that commitment against great odds. But it is not easy for pastors who are trying to incorporate the intellectual love of God in their ministries because anti-intellectualism in the Black church is pervasive. We just want to sing and pray and preach and tell the story of how we got over the hill and through the valley. Blacks like to celebrate their faith, clap their hands, and stamp their feet so they can have a good time as they praise the Lord for having brought them a mighty long way. Therefore, it is hard for Black pastors to find the time to read and write and reflect. Every Black pastor I know who is a serious student of theology complains of how difficult it is to get their peers and congregations to understand that a pastor needs time to study, not just for sermon preparation, but for knowledge on how to make the gospel understandable for the time and situation in which we are living today.

What is it that we need to know about the gospel and the world so we can become more effective witnesses of Jesus Christ and become creative change in society? Wars are rampant in Iraq, in Afghanistan, on the continent of Africa, in Europe, in Latin America, and all around the world. One hundred million people were killed by their brothers in the twentieth century. And at the rate we have started the twenty-first century, we will top that if we live long enough to tell the tale of our self-destruction.

When considering what the Black church should know to become creative agents of change in today's world, we must look at the nearly four-hundred-year-long history of terror against Black people in the United States. We have endured slavery and survived Jim Crow, segregation, and lynching, and today we are fighting police brutality throughout the streets of America. The criminal justice system is locking up Black people in prisons and jails at such a rapid rate that half of the incarcerated today are Black. We are 50 percent of the prison population and only about 12 percent of the general population.

The terror of AIDS is destroying the people in our communities, in Africa, and throughout the world at a staggering rate. Forty million people are infected with this horrible disease, and three-fourths—thirty million of them—are in Africa. The Black church has been slow to address the AIDS crisis in our community because we have a misunderstanding of the relationship between the Christian faith and sexuality, which hinders an intelligent and creative approach to deal with the problem. We were also slow to address patriarchy in the church, women in the ministry, and homophobia. Why is it that the Black church can be so progressive on race and so conservative when dealing with patriarchy and homophobia? Why does the Black church not have a better response to these issues?

One reason is that we have a backward theology, which we borrowed from white evangelicals. It is a dualistic theology that separates the soul from the body; male from female; spirituality from sexuality. This misguided, dualistic theology proclaims one side good and holy and the other side bad and evil. We need to have knowledge—sophisticated knowledge—to recognize this dualism and then create a theology that struggles against these oppressive attitudes.

What is the prophetic word of ministry to the African American community and to America and to the world? What are we going to say about this terrible human predicament—about all of the hurt, the pain, and the suffering that people endure today? Ministers need to do more than just read the Bible to answer these problems. Ministers need to study. Sincerity is not enough. If sincerity is not buffered with intelligence, it can become a very destructive force in society.

The Black church needs all of the intellectual and spiritual resources we can muster in order to cope with the complex and dangerous world we live in. Do not underestimate evil's power to confuse and corrupt the mind and the spirit. We are struggling not just against flesh and blood, not just against an individual instance of oppression, but against structural evil.

As ministers reflect on their vocation and calling, I encourage them to ask these crucial questions: What is your congregation's calling, and what do you need to do to help them fulfill it? What is your calling, and how can your congregation empower you to fulfill it? Is the intellectual component of the ministry as important for your congregation as it is for you? Clarity about your vocation—what it means for you and for the people you are serving—is indispensable for living out your vocation effectively.

I have struggled with the question of my vocation all of my life, and I return continually to the time and the place when I first heard my call to the ministry. It was during my first year in college. I was only sixteen—a little early to feel and to respond to such a monumental calling. At first, I thought it was a call to the pastoral ministry. But in seminary I discovered that God was calling me to teach preachers. I just could not stop reading books, raising critical questions about why we say we believe one thing and yet do another. I first saw the contradiction in terms of race through examining the relations between Black and white people in Arkansas. I just could not understand how white Christians could say they believed in God and in segregation. I did not understand how white Christians could treat Black people with no regard for their rights as human beings.

Then I saw a similar contradiction in Black churches—people who said they loved God but participated in all kinds of corruption in the church itself. Corruption in Black churches troubles me deeply; ministers, deacons, stewards—so-called Christians—act as if they own the church. These contradictions pushed me to search for a deeper understanding of God and humanity, of faith and love, so that the people would not confuse a corrupt Christianity with the real thing. I became obsessed with the need to understand the difference between the Christianity in its true sense and its counterfeit version. That was why I became a theologian.

The question that we must answer is what is God calling us to do in the church and in society, and how must we do it? If you are called to be a pastor, be the best pastor you can be. Urge your congregation to provide you with the material support, the free time to think, and the open space to do what God has called you to do.

A calling is like a spiritual obsession—something that possesses you to the extent that you cannot turn away from it. It defines your every move, shapes your spiritual and committed provision, and sets your priorities.

Consider the calling, or spiritual obsession, of many of our heroes. Rosa Parks refused to give up her seat and move to the back of the bus. Her refusal started the Civil Rights revolution among the Black masses and transformed America. God called twenty-six-year-old Martin Luther King Jr. to lead that Black freedom struggle. King became so obsessed with the calling to bring justice to the land that nothing could stop him except an assassin's bullet. King's philosophy and spirit live on in the world today and call us to make real the ideal of the beloved humankind.

Malcolm X received his calling in jail. He was possessed by a kind of Black righteousness. It was a divine calling to make Blackness a thing of beauty, a joy to behold, something to love and to admire, and to be proud of because we are God's beautiful African creatures. As King taught us to love white people even though they hated us, Malcolm rebuked him and said that before Blacks can love anybody they must first love themselves, and he was right. The Second Commandment says to love the neighbor as much as we love ourselves. The love of self, therefore, is the first law, and loving the neighbor is the second. Many Blacks did not want to hear Malcolm's message about Blackness, and, like King, Malcolm too was assassinated. And even though both prophets knew they were going to be killed, they could not turn away from their calling.

James Baldwin was a young Harlem Pentecostal preacher who only finished high school. But when God got ahold of his mind, his intellectual imagination, Baldwin wrote like an angel. Baldwin's ministry in words gave us hope that we would overcome because love is greater than hate. When God lays a hand on you and sets you aside for the ministry of words, there is no way to escape.

The Bible is filled with characters trying to run away from a divine calling. Moses could not escape when God selected him for a ministry of liberation. Moses tried to run away from the call, but God caught up with him. I have seen the misery of my people, God told Moses. Go tell Pharaoh that the time for oppression is over. Moses tried to get out of his calling—as many of us do—complaining that he did not know God's name and that he could not speak well and that he was not eloquent and that nobody would believe him. But God always has a way to answer any excuse that we may have to escape the calling.

Jonah tried to get away because he did not want to go to Nineveh to preach to people he did not like. But God caught up with him, too.

The power of God possessed each of these heroes of faith and compelled them to fight for justice and to ask critical and relevant questions about the world they lived in. God's power was the something within each of them that forced them to answer their call to serve as priests and prophets. The same spirit empowered these faithful servants to love God with their hearts, minds, and souls. We are called to follow their lead.

6.

Liberating the Ancient Utterances of African People

Asa G. Hilliard III

TODAY'S PROPHETS AND CHURCH LEADERS are called to communicate the truth of a living way to a people fascinated unto death, a people who do not know their culture. The captivity that truly holds us in place is fundamentally cultural, and yet often we do not understand the connection between culture and captivity. We know we hurt, but we don't know how we were hurt. Captivity continues today; we are not free yet.

How is it possible that, after we've been freed so many times—through Civil Rights legislation, Emancipation, and so forth—we're still in slavery? I believe that at any time we choose, we can turn the key on the lock and be free. In order to be free or to have the desire to be free, we need to understand the magnitude of our captivity. In 1918 George Wells Parker, one of our great historians, described in one paragraph the whole history of African people. He wrote:

> In the morning of the world when the fingers of love swept aside the curtain of time, our dusty mother, Ethiopia, held the stage. It was she who wooed civilization and gave birth to nations. Egypt was her firstborn. . . . religion, art, literature, science, and civilization are hers (Ethiopia's). An eternity but lived in the warmth of her radiant glow. I have chosen to call the unnumbered millions of her descendents children of the sun.[1]

Parker describes the development of civilization. He describes Ethiopia as the mother of civilization and Egypt as her most successful child. Then he summarizes the impact of the Nile Valley on the spread of body, thought, and behavior throughout the rest of the known world.

Part of what keeps us in captivity is that we haven't understood the role that we played in the beginning of civilization in all of its aspects. This is what made Ayi Kwei Armah write in *Two Thousand Seasons*:

> We are not a people of yesterday. Do not ask how many single seasons we have flowed from our beginning until now. . . . Count all of the stars in the sky. . . . Then after they have reached the end of that counting, we shall not ask them to number the rain drops in the ocean, but with the wisdom of the aftermath of that counting, then ask again: How many seasons have flowed since our people were unborn?[2]

Most of our people don't see ourselves as Armah describes. We see ourselves as a local, temporal people in a global world full of antiquity except for us and our story. Therefore, prophets and today's church leaders are called to link memory with fore-listening, to join the uncountable seasons of our flowing to the unknown tomorrows. We are called to pass on the truth of our origins to a people rushing death-ward, grown contemptuous of our ignorance of our source and prejudiced against our own survival. How shall your vocational utterance be heard?

As we work to set our captives free from denying our nature, consider the following two different worldviews. Sobonfu Somé tells a simple story; she and her husband, Malidoma Somé, are Dagara people. In the Foreword to Sobonfu Somé's book *Welcoming Spirit Home* Brooke Medicine Eagle describes the birth of a child in the Dagara community in this way:

> A child is born. S/he comes into the world of nature, perhaps in a simple structure where bird song can be heard. The breath of life is blown into her nostrils by a midwife. The child draws upon herself in this new world. A loving and supportive embrace of mother and family surround her from the first moment. There are more people who want to hold her than there are hours in the day. . . . The people around her in the community know how to get along well and she learns these ways of relationship with ease.

Love fills her day before she has a word for love. Often, she's with her grandparents and with other elders who share the stories of the family and the wisdom of her people. . . . Her elders watch her and give her a tantalizing array of experiences and choices so that her natural tendencies and gifts begin to show themselves. They look deeply into her spirit with their wise spirit-filled eyes and what she loves and who she is becomes purely evident and the uniqueness of her contribution to the people is seen and named and nurtured. The only code of the village is to support the highest intention and the finest being of each person. . . . She becomes masterful at what she loves and offers the great gift to her people from her heart through her hands.[3]

Now consider the second worldview, that of a child born in the United States.

The child comes into the glaring brightness in a room with no windows, surrounded by the smell of chemicals. Her basic instinct is to be frightened for her mother's heartbeat has changed. . . . When she passes through into the light of her own day, she's taken from her mother where she most needs the reassurance from lying on that familiar heartbeat. Something stings her eyes and she's alone. Her crying brings no response and she finally falls into exhausted sleep to wake up again alone in a crib. When she finally goes home with her mother, she's still alone much of the time. Her mother is alone and exhausted. . . . There is no one there to help her. Before very long the baby is left all day in a strange place with a stranger who is busy with many other stressed and crying babies. . . . The child draws into herself in a certain way. Her wishes feel like demands that are not being met and hurt and anger enter before she has words for those. . . . At night, television entertains her. Finally, the whole family is together around TV where someone else's life or fiction or violence has been given her and she grows up not knowing who she is. An adult has to drive her everywhere. In school she is asked to sit still, to be quiet and to control her natural tendencies and interests. Her aliveness is dampened into obedience. . . . Her rhythm is tuned to somebody else's needs. . . . She tries to pick some job she would like to do in her life. It doesn't work out for her so well because her days are dead-ended and dull. Loud music and stimulants, coffee and stronger things help sometimes, but not for long.[4]

These descriptions detail the lives of two children with two different worldviews, two different ways of thinking about what a human being is, two ways of thinking about human relationships and their value, about spirit versus materialism, and so forth.

Part of the worldview of African people all over the continent is to replicate the first description. My friend Dr. Fuchiowe, who is from the Congo, says that when a child is born in the Congo, the whole community says, "A living sun, a part of God, has come to us. Now our job is to treat this living son like God him/herself." This affirmation from the entire community shapes the everyday lives of the children.

An African worldview is derived from deep study of everything in the environment, including the weather, stars, animals, agriculture, and each other. At the end of that study of the environment, almost all Africans believe that God has given us a book, and the thing that we study is that book. And, if we study it hard enough, God's principles and values will be revealed in what we see. Out of that the core principle that permeates the worldview of Africans—even though they have different names for it and different places—is a value system that sums up in one word everything that they have learned. That value system is called Maat. In some places, they call it mojo, which is where we get the phrase: "I've got my mojo working." (Unfortunately, we're so uninformed about who we are that we don't even know the origin of the words we use.) Maat is one of the highest statements of an ancient African value system. It takes seven English words to sum up Maat: truth, justice, order, harmony, balance, reciprocity, and righteousness. You don't study Maat; you must be Maat.

This value system has arisen because everything they see in nature is harmony and balance. Out of this way of seeing the world some Africans name the behaviors that would match the value system of Maat. And in the ancient Nile Valley Africans had forty-two things they had to say in order to show that they had actually done Maat. These forty-two things are called by some people the negative confessions, but Africans have given them the name "the declarations of virtue." Some will sound familiar: "I have not done wrong. I have not robbed with violence. I have not done wickedness to anyone. I have not commissioned theft. I have not acted deceitfully. I have not robbed the things that belong to God. I have told no lies. . . ."

Our version of these declarations is condensed in the Ten Commandments. These Nile Valley virtues are part of the things that Moses studied, according to Acts 7:22. Moses was an Egyptian priest learned in all the wisdom of ancient Egypt. The Egyptians believed that after they die and stand before God, their heart must be weighed in the balance against truth; if their heart and truth match, they can be led by the Son of God to the throne of God. Depictions of the heart-weighing scenes are found in the oldest sacred text, whose name means "coming forth from darkness into light." When the Germans found this sacred text, however, they called it "The Book of the Dead." But that's not what the Africans called the text. Let them speak for themselves.

In the book of the coming forth from darkness into light, our ancestors speak about how they understood their relationship to the Creator. Below is a composite list of how our ancestors describe God in this sacred text:

> God is one and alone, and none other existeth with him. God is the One, the One who hath made all things. . . . God is from the beginning, and He hath been from the beginning. He hath existed from old and was when nothing else had being. . . . God is the Eternal One. He is eternal and infinite and endureth forever. . . . No man knoweth His form. No man hath been able to seek out His likeness. . . . His names are innumerable. . . . God is truth and He feedeth thereon. . . . God is life and through Him only man liveth. . . . God hath stretched out the heavens and founded the earth. What His heart conceived straightway came to pass, and when He hath spoken it cometh to pass and endureth forever. . . . God is merciful unto those who reverence Him and He heareth him that calleth upon Him. God knoweth him that acknowledges Him; He rewardeth him that serveth Him, and He protecteth him that followeth Him.[5]

This text shows Africans understood God five thousand to six thousand years ago and before. We haven't heard about those Africans; we've heard about "primitives," "savages," and "pagans," but we have not heard from the people themselves.

In order to understand what captivity means, you have to know what you left behind because people took a lot of our stuff when we went into captivity.

A Zulu—Jordan I. Nuboni—said that when he was a teenager, his father took him through an initiation process that all Zulus go through, and his father then passed along Zulu understanding of the world. One of the things that his father made him do was to memorize the fundamental understanding of how they saw the world. In paraphrase this is what he memorized: "I am. I am alive. I am conscious and aware. I am unique. I am who I say I am. I am the value of God—the deity. I am the face of humanity. Form is an unchanging value. Value is eternal consciousness. Consciousness is that in which all things have their origin. It does not change. It is a part of God. I am a part of God. I am the consciousness. The infinity is a unity. It cannot be destroyed. I am a constituent of this unity. I cannot be destroyed. The infinity and I are inseparable. I cannot exist outside this infinity, for there is no outside of it. The infinity is alive. There is no death within it. That which is alive has purpose. Purpose is destiny. Perpetual evolution is the destiny of God."

The final part of the Zulu rites of passage affirmation includes the following: "I know every one of my cells. My mother taught me how to count them. My mother is mother of all women. All women are my mother. I prostrate myself before all women. All men, I cry, arise. Fathers of the person create the world in which it will be no crime to be your children. I know I shall prevail because I am who I say I am. He has not been born who can say that he conquered me." This affirmation comes from a Zulu view of the world, and it demonstrates the importance of studying customs and traditions from all over the continent to understand who Africans are.

As we sample African culture, we also find out where we get mathematics, science, technology, philosophy, and other fields of knowledge. The National Council of Teachers of Mathematics in America uses an African textbook as a part of its archives. The council has to use it because it is the oldest mathematics textbook on the earth. The textbook was written approximately two thousand years before the birth of Christ. Problems in trigonometry—not just geometry and algebra—are found in this ancient African textbook, dated fifteen hundred years before Pythagoras.

But one of the most awesome things about the document is that it describes six steps in the scientific method. So Greece, whatever it did with the scientific method, repeated what Africans had already done; the Greeks picked up whatever they had studied with the teachers in the Nile Valley. The scientific method includes a response to one word that is also found in 2000 B.C.E. That word is called *sba*. To translate an African word to a Greek word, substitute *ph* for *b*, which would give you *spha*, which becomes *sophi* or *sophia*—or *wisdom*—the deep understanding of things. Greeks learned philosophy in the Nile Valley from African teachers and priests, and Greeks went back home and used that very term—not a Greek term—to name the thing that meant more to them than anything. The Africans had an understanding of God. These Africans had spirit, and these Africans were hurt by the first faith-based initiative. If Greek people respected what the Africans had to say, they could have "bussed" themselves to integrate into this system.

Romans were interested in power. Constantine, who convened the Council of Nicaea, had already been a murderer. But Constantine had a peculiar interpretation of the cross. He said by this sign—the cross— conquer! He didn't mean conquer souls; he meant take land and kill people in the name of God. People frequently hijack Christian institutions for nefarious purposes, which turns into an interesting faith-based initiative.

Consider Leopold of Belgium as an example of what happened to African people, beginning in East Africa with the Portuguese. Leopold of Belgium wrote to the preachers about what his intentions were and what he needed to do and why. Paraphrasing Leopold's instructions will give us an angle on their myopia:

> The task that is given to fulfill is a very delicate task and requires much tact. You will go certainly to evangelize, but your evangelization must inspire above all Belgium interests. Your principle objective of our mission in the Congo is never to teach the Congolese to know God. This they know already. They speak and submit to a God. One calls him Mongo. The other calls him Zambi. They know that to kill or to sleep with someone else's wife, to lie, to insult is bad. Your essential role is to facilitate the task of administrators and industrialists, which means you will interpret the gospel in a way that will be best to protect your interests in that part of the world. For these things you have to keep watch on disinteresting our savages from the riches that are plentiful in their competition and dreams or else they will be competitive and overthrow you. So, you've got to preach a gospel that says that wealth is bad. Your knowledge of the gospel will allow you to find text ordering and encouraging your followers to love poverty like: happy are the poor because they will inherit heaven. Make them disrespect everything which gives courage to affront us. Your actions will be directed essentially to the younger ones.

In other words, Leopold told the preachers: "Please, leave no child behind." He continued:

> Convert always the black by using the whip. Keep their women in nine months of submission to work freely or force to pay

you in signs of recognition—goats, chicken and eggs every time you visit their villages and be sure that they never become rich. Saying every day that it is impossible for the rich to enter heaven. Institute a confessional system that allows you to be good detectives denouncing any black that has made a different consciousness contrary to that of the decision maker. Teach them to forget their heroes and to adore ours only.

This was a plan. It sounds like a plan for captivity. One of the things I found about captivity is captives get affected in interesting ways.

An article about American hostages held in Iran reported that when the hostages were enslaved, they exhibited anger and irregular heartbeats. They became irritable, insomniac, melancholy, nauseous, depressed, and so forth. However, when asked how they were treated, they reply, "well." This reaction is called the Stockholm syndrome. "How did the captors treat you?" "They treated us good!"

There are people saying right now that the people who have us in captivity are treating us "good." You think they get to mix and mingle and talk and converse? That's the worst thing that could happen from the point of view of the captor. Require them to ask permission for simple things like going to the toilet so they will have a subordinate understanding of themselves. Depersonalize them in every way. Restrict the captive's conversation to captors only. Give breaks for smoking as a reward. Rotate the guards so they have no chance to bond with the guard. Make hostages totally dependent. Keep hostages under the constant threat of death. Destroy the unity of the hostages. Control, above all, information going to the hostages. Keep them in the dark.

How do hostages resist? In news reports of what happened to those hostages in Iran, some defended themselves when they realized what was happening by taking charge of whatever space they had and making themselves directors of their own space. They read poetry to themselves. They played word games in their head. They wrote long letters to people. They sought independence and self-control by any means necessary. They used their own words rather than the words of their captors. Unfortunately, many people cannot wait to learn the words of the captor, because they know they will benefit. They use their own initiative, and they use their own leadership.

Robinson Crusoe said about his "man Friday": "I smiled at him and looked pleasantly. I beckoned to him to come nearer. At length he came close to me. Then he kneeled down again. He kissed the ground. He laid his head on the ground and took me by the foot and set my foot on his head. This it seemed to me was a token of swearing to me to be my slave forever."[6]

"To be my slave forever" is an agenda. Some people think we were free with the Civil Rights Act and the Emancipation Proclamation. We're not out. We're not out because the plan—the agenda—is to put us deeper in. Martin Luther King Jr. said, "If we are to get on the right side of the world revolution, we as a nation must undergo a radical revolution of values. . . . When machines and computers, profit motives and property rights are considered more important than people, the giant triplets of racism, materialism, and militarism are incapable of being conquered."[7] There is a value problem in America; we are not talking about Maat values here.

In his book *The Grand Chessboard* Zbigniew Brzezinski says:

> The overseas British Empire was initially acquired through a combination of exploitation, trade and conquest. But, much like its Roman and Chinese predecessors or French and Spanish rivals, it derived a great deal of its staying power from the perception of British cultural superiority. That superiority was not only a matter of subjective arrogance on the part of the imperial ruling class, but was a perspective shared by many of the non-British subjects. Cultural superiority successfully asserted and by the victim quietly conceded had the effect of reducing [the conquered] to rely on a large military force to maintain the power of the imperial centos.[8]

What do Brzezinski's words have to do with us today, as we try to hear the utterances from our African ancestors for liberation? I know I remember coming up in church, and it always felt holier for me to say thee, thou, and thine, even though Jesus never spoke English to my knowledge. But we get holy by having an older form of English because British people in their language thought it was holier. That's a naive view, however. Somebody is trying to rule the world. That's what *The Grand Chessboard* is about. Former President George H. W. Bush named the Middle East as the place that the United States should control, before his son, George W. Bush, got in power with the same agenda. It is important that we know what the game is that is being played because we're a part of the game.

Brzezinski says, "A power that dominates Eurasia will control two of the world's three most advanced economically productive areas. And, a mere glance at the map also suggests that control over Eurasia will almost automatically entail Africa's subordination."[9] Brzezenski is not talking about putting handcuffs on you. He's not talking about the chain on your leg or about the radio control thing that monitors where you are. We have better ways to control a population. All we need is to put the chains on the mind so that the people do not know what it means to be whole; they do not know who they are or where they came from; they do not know their cultural heritage; they do not know the agenda of their captors; they do not know the consequences of captivity on their minds and spirits and do not know the structure of global political economy. The people do not know the nature of strategic propaganda, which is as simple as the picture of Christ. The white, blond-haired Jesus is one I had on my fan. And it is the one in the movie. However, I found another one—a much different one—and it's the oldest picture of Christ that I've ever seen. It is in the third century in a Roman catacomb, and it is what Jesus used to look like to the Romans. How did the artist Rembrandt's idea develop and become popular a thousand years later? Well, you say it doesn't matter: Christ is colorless. Well, then, paint him Black—how he looked to the Romans.

In conclusion, I suggest we consider the pandemic crisis of AIDS—Acquired Immune Deficiency Syndrome. We know what AIDS is—a debilitating and ultimately fatal disease. At present, African people all over the world are at highest risk. This virus spreads through intimate social union, through exposure to blood products and infected persons, and it destroys the protection normally present in the human body—the immune system. Without a functioning immune system, the human body is vulnerable, ultimately weakening, and unable to survive. Our survival is threatened by the pandemic of AIDS.

Something else as deadly as AIDS threatens our very existence as a people. Another acquired immune deficiency—cultural AIDS—is a virus infecting our people. Our mental universe, our worldview, our critical consciousness, our virtues are at the core of our being and are as much a part of who we are as is our physical universe. Our social, cultural, and ethnic bonds as a people are part of our universe, and they are the bonds that make us a people. Without them we cease to exist. We are strong as a people when we are cohesive. Cohesiveness arises because of bonds produced by shared culture. Without ethnic bonds, we cease to exist as a family.

All great and powerful people in the world today manifest that cohesiveness. They invest heavily in the nurture, enhancement, and protection of these bonds—even to the extent of creating a world war to do it. Some ethnic groups have even gone beyond the physical wars to declare on us cultural wars. Books are written to destroy the culture of anybody who competes on their own—even if you're not trying to sell your culture.

In *The Clash of Civilizations* Samuel P. Huntington writes about how to take over the world, how to understand Arabic culture, and how the European world can understand Islam. Huntington also wrote a book called *Cultural Matters*, which says that African nations are failing because they have bad culture. In *No Excuses* two Harvard professors write that African children in America don't learn because the community has bad culture. The culture wars are on, but we have culture surrender in our own community. We have to pay at least as much attention to cultural AIDS as to physical AIDS. We started out in the way that they described Ethiopia in the beginning: we ran into myopia—cool, cold-blooded, and calculated. And we know how the system works and that it targeted our consciousness as the target—and really the ultimate target is our spirit, our soul. We cannot function in ignorance of the strategy. But once we're conscious, at any moment we choose, we can free ourselves because we have the key in our pocket to unlock the cell that we're in, and we can walk off free on our own initiative. As Harriet Tubman said, "Yes, I did free hundreds of slaves, but I could have freed thousands if only they had known they were slaves."

7.

The Prophetic Imperative

Reclaiming the Gospel
by Speaking Truth to Power

*An abridged transcript of remarks by
Obery M. Hendricks Jr.*

OUR CONFERENCE THEME IS "Setting the Captives Free." When we talk about freedom and liberation, we're not just talking in the narrow hyper-spiritualized sense; we're speaking in the holistic sense in which Jesus spoke—setting free those in economic, political, social, and spiritual bondage.

Generally speaking, our churches today are so engaged in hyper-spiritualizing worship, building churches into big businesses, and turning themselves into gospel entertainment centers, that we sometimes lose sight of the real mandate of the gospel. In this sense, our focus is often fixed on "Church-ianity" rather than Christianity.

Church-ianity is a solitary focus on what goes in the local church or denomination; what goes on in the rest of the world is secondary, to the extent that it gets any attention at all. Church-ianity's concern is institutional maintenance rather than ministering to the world. Church-ianity lacks a holistic view of spirituality. Jesus said, Love your Lord your God, with all your heart, soul, mind, and strength. But that is only part of the pronouncement. He also told us to love our neighbors as ourselves. The love Jesus prescribes is not love as mere sentiment. It doesn't mean to "get up and give somebody a holy hug." The love that Jesus speaks of is not just something you feel; it's what you do. This is holistic spirituality. Its reach is both vertical (to God) and horizontal (to humanity). Holistic spirituality means having a personal relationship with God and, as the expression of that relationship, striving to make the kind of world in which our neighbors can have the same degree of health, happiness, freedom, and wholeness that we want for as ourselves.

That's holistic spirituality. It is the spirituality that looks outside of our narrow personal and organizational concerns and instead seeks to transform the world into the world of justice and peace and wholeness that God wills. That is the difference between true Christianity and Church-ianity: Christianity calls us to change the world, not to just grow churches. It calls us to strive to make every principality and power just and righteous, to bring low every structure of oppression, exploitation, and fear.

Yet today too often our actions seem to say, "Just give us the church and the devil can have the world." That is the essence of Church-ianity, and that is why it is blasphemy, even idolatry: because under the guise of the gospel we worship our own comfort and desires instead of the clear commandments of Christ. What is needed is not Church-ianity, but holistic spirituality. That is what the Church of Christ is built upon.

On the day of Pentecost, a group of Jesus' followers were scared to death, hiding in the upper room because they were frightened that they might be tortured and murdered like Jesus. Then the Holy Spirit came down upon them like tongues of fire. And when the Holy Spirit lit upon them, all of a sudden they weren't thinking about hanging out in the church all the time anymore. When the Spirit of God came upon them, they went out to change the world. That's holistic spirituality. And that's how you know if you're really Spirit-filled: you can't wait to go out and change the world.

That's important because these days folks seem to think that spirituality is only vertical, that is, between them and God alone. They conveniently forget the part about loving your neighbor. That's why folks can get up in church and testify, "Oh, he's my all and all," then sit back down and not even speak to the person sitting next to them, or, worse, step right over the hungry person outside the church. And, Lord have mercy, don't let somebody come into the church dressed differently than we think they should be dressed!

Most of us have exhibited these kinds of thoughts and feelings from time to time because that's the way we were raised. But, our call is to change this thing. That's what this conference is about: becoming catalysts for change. And that's what we're called to be as servants of the gospel: agents of just and righteous change in this world.

Our theme, "Setting the Captives Free," comes from Jesus' para-phrasing of Isaiah 61 in Luke 4:18-19, which is the inaugural sermon of Jesus' ministry. In this first sermon, Jesus stated who he was and what he was about—a sermon that seems to be overlooked too often. Jesus said: "The Spirit of the Lord is upon me—" not because it makes him shout or do the holy dance. He says, "The Spirit of the Lord is upon me, because he has anointed me to bring good news to the poor. He has sent me to proclaim release to the captives and recovery of sight to the blind, to let the oppressed go free, to proclaim the year of the Lord's favor."

What is Jesus' good news to the poor? It is the good news that Jesus' ministry has set in motion a transformation of the systems and social orders that keep people poor no matter how hard they work, and beat them down so badly that Jesus had to pronounce a beatitude upon them to remind them that they are blessed; a system that has some folk living large for generations like it is their due, while others struggle just to survive. The good news of Jesus is that that kind of system, that kind of world, cannot forever stand, and won't stand much longer if folk accept the full radicality of his message. Good news means a change from the bad news of poverty and exploitation. This is a politi-cal pronouncement with unquestionable economic overtones.

"He has sent me to proclaim release to the captives." In Roman-occupied Jewish Palestine during the time of Jesus, the prisons basi-cally were full of two types: those who were suspected of insurrection against the government (these didn't stay in prison long; they were usually executed); and debtors, folks who had defaulted on debts that in many cases were the result of oppressive levels of imperial taxation. It was these who comprised most of those held in the prisons. They were captives, but they were not criminals.

So Jesus was talking about proclaiming release to those who were in captivity to an unjust political order. That is a political pronounce-ment. It's an important point to keep in mind today when the prison-industrial complex in America continues to flourish under President George W. Bush. I don't know if President Bush is personally evil, but I know what he's doing is evil. That's right, evil. It is evil because it is unjust. It's not just politics—it's evil. One of the things we have to start doing is calling things as they are. Christians can be so mealy-mouthed. Part of the reason for that is because we're raised right. We're raised to be polite, to not badmouth others. That's important. I taught my children that, too. But we can't let our polite upbring-ings make us forget what it means to be a prophet with a prophetic imperative. We must speak the truth. If something is evil, we must call it evil. Anything less is an abdication of our responsibility as followers of the Messiah.

"Recovery of sight for the blind" can, of course, refer to spiritual blindness. But it can also mean physical blindness. Jesus healed physical blindness. But physical blindness has social and political significance because much of that blindness was the result of malnutrition and disease which, in turn, were results of poverty and living in impoverished circumstances. Healing conditions that are the result of poverty implies also healing the system that causes the poverty. So the phrase "recovery of sight to the blind" has a socioeconomic and political meaning as well.

The next mandate, "to set at liberty those who are oppressed," doesn't need a long exegesis. But it is important to note that *thlipsis*, the Greek word for *oppressed* means pressed down, weighed down by bondage. I want to make that clear. It does not mean bruised or tribulation, either of which can simply denote a skin boil or shoes that are too tight. The term connotes political oppression, that is, pressed down and held down by those who unjustly wield political power.

"To proclaim the acceptable year of the Lord" seems clearly to refer to the jubilee year, the end of the fifty-year cycle in which all debts are forgiven and any land that has been expropriated as a result of debt is returned to its rightful owners. That is how most biblical commentators understand it. Its meaning is overtly political.

This was Jesus' initial sermon—his inaugural sermon—by which he announced to the world who he was and what he came to do. I presented this sermon to you in social and political and economic terms, as a radical manifesto for world transformation. It seems clear that is what Jesus intended. But that devalues the spirituality of Jesus' ministry because spirituality is about how we treat our neighbor, about how we act in the world. In other words, how we act in the world is the only real measure of our spirituality; it is the only way we can know if we're truly spiritual. If it is not about how we act toward others, then what we call spirituality is just feelings and emotional sensations we have deluded ourselves to believe is spirituality. I know sometimes things feel spiritual. But we must remember that feelings, no matter how spiritual they seem to be, are still in the realm of the senses and sensuality. Feelings are a fleeting state and they can change and they do change. Ultimately, it is our actions that count. That is the measure of true spirituality. Apparently for Jesus freeing the poor and oppressed was a large part of the spiritual meaning of his ministry.

One of the areas in which today's churches should exercise caution is the area of praise and praise services. It is important to realize that a good, emotionally charged praise service is only part of what true praise is about. Too often praise just changes the way people feel without inspiring them to do anything differently. If praise doesn't cause you to do anything different, then you have to question its spiritual content.

The reason some churches feature emotionally charged praise services is because if they do not, people are going to leave and go to churches where they can get that worked-up feeling. So, to keep their members and to attract new ones, these churches focus on the praise hour to the point that it almost becomes the entertainment hour. In my article, "The Problem With Gospel Music Today,"[1] I quoted a past president of the Gospel Music Association, who spoke approvingly of the entertainment value of gospel music in churches. The tragedy of his assessment was that he didn't see anything wrong with entertainment in the church. This presents a real paradox because, on the one hand, you can't have an impact on folk if you don't have them in your house, and one way you can be sure to get them there is to entertain them. On the other hand, if you do give in to the entertainment impulse, you're allowing yourself to be driven by numbers rather than by the quality of the gospel message God has entrusted to you.

Despite these concerns, I contend that church folk want so very much to be empowered. They are so tired of the messy world we're living in that they would gladly cleave to a prophetic biblical perspective that speaks truth to power if they are given the chance. They would hold fast to an empowering preacher/teacher whose witness makes a difference in the every day political and economic environment of their lives, not just in church and not just on Sunday.

But a prophetic ministry has to be uncompromising. At some point we might have to take a hit, maybe even experience a drop in membership, in order to reconfigure our ministries so that they are in line with what the gospel would have us do. Now, I know this is a hard paradigm because no one wants to take the chance of being in the pulpit talking to himself or herself. But the measure of successful ministry is not in numbers. Jesus only had twelve followers and all of them weren't right. The scriptures say that on several occasions he had five thousand people listening to him. But most of the time, Jesus went around to little villages that had only a handful of people. During his lifetime he did not have great numbers behind him, but that was not his concern. His concern was to utter truths in season and out of season, because he knew that in God's time that is what will transform the world. His focus was the legacy of his faithful struggle, not the glory of great numbers cheering him on.

We see this most clearly in the gospel of Mark, in which Jesus is always on the way. He is always going out trying to spread the word, trying to make a difference in the people's lives. For us, going out means stepping outside our comfort zones, stepping outside our churches. I'm not talking about going out and preaching revivals; I mean going out and struggling against injustice. We as servants of Christ are supposed to be the vanguard of society. We are the ones who are supposed to influence the definitions and directions, but we can't do that by staying holed up in the church around folk who are Amen-ing us all the time. That's not Jesus' way. His way is to go out and confront the world. That doesn't mean you have to go out and march; there are all kinds of ways to effect change. Go to city council meetings. Go to rallies. Write letters, make phone calls, make yourself heard at forums that affect the people's welfare and quality of life. Most of all, make sure that those entrusted to you are made aware of the issues that affect their lives.

A few years ago I had occasion to speak at Allen Temple Baptist Church in Oakland, California, which is led by that great scholar-pastor, Dr. J. Alfred Smith. What really impressed me was that during the time for announcements and notices, amid reports of bake sales and official board meetings, designated members stood up and talked about pending political issues. They raised people's consciences about happenings on the national and local scene. They shared which policies were passed, which cases are before the Supreme Court, and what people should be concerned about. They encouraged congregants to attend this political meeting, to write to that congressperson, to email this one or the other one. They actually had political action committees within the church to raise people's political consciousness and awareness. This is an example of the gospel in action. It makes a difference. We, too, can do this at any time. Allow a group of members to speak about political action and awareness at each service and, little by little, you'll have an informed congregation energized to do their part to help establish God's kingdom of justice on earth, as in heaven.

So it is important that we let our people know that the gospel is innately political. That's not all it is, of course, but it is political, too. Anyone who doesn't understand this doesn't understand the gospel. Think about it. The central figure of our faith was executed on a political charge—crucifixion was reserved for those found guilty of rebellion against the Roman state. In other words, he was executed as a revolutionary. Yet many Christians today only talk about the fact that Jesus came to save souls. Yes, he did come to save souls. But that's not all he came to save. To only be concerned about saving souls while ignoring people's physical suffering and bondage is a narrow approach to salvation indeed. Somehow, it seems to lack compassion. But to acknowledge that we have a savior who died a political death—that tells us something. And what it tells us is the salvation Jesus lived and died to bring to us is not only heavenly, but it has an earthly dimension, too. It is innately political. We have to help our people come to see that.

As we each reflect upon about our own calls to ministry, we have to define what it really means to be a prophet and to be prophetic. We usually think of foretelling as the only measure of prophesy. Foretelling is a part of prophecy, but it is the second part and the lesser part, at that. The biblical prophet tells us, "This is what you're doing wrong and this is what you should be doing, and if you don't obey, if you don't do what the Lord says, then so-and-so of the Lord's judgment will befall you." This is foretelling. But the core of prophecy is forth-telling, telling the truth of God because God has said so: "Thus saith the Lord," was the prophets' mantra. The core of prophecy is critiquing the injustices, the wrongheadedness, the political and social evils bedeviling the social order. Look at what the prophets did. They stood up and spoke out against what was going on in society. They used good judgment, they weren't reckless, but they didn't count the cost. They chose where they spoke and made sure they were speaking to whom they should speak, but they did not jockey around to find the safest spots and the points of least resistance. They spoke the truth of God as they knew it and were faithful to their calling.

But, yes, there is a price to be paid for prophesying. There is no cheap grace. It is free, but it is not cheap. The gospel is a radical thing. And so is prophesying. That is why there can be no such thing as a conservative prophet. Prophets do not seek to conserve the social order; their goal is to change it, to make it more just. It is important to remember this in a time when so many of us have declared ourselves to be political conservatives. There is a difference between moral conservatism and political conservatism. But those in control love to fool us into thinking they are the same thing.

No one was more morally conservative than my mother. But politically she and the arch-conservative Jessie Helms didn't have a thing in common. Political conservatives seek to preserve the privilege and power of those who already have wealth and power. A clear-eyed perusal of the historical record will easily verify this fact. That is not what prophetic Christianity stands for. Political conservatism is the exact opposite of prophetic Christianity. That's why you cannot be aligned with politically conservative forces in a society and still be fulfilling the prophetic mandate of the gospel. This point cannot be stressed enough. If you have a problem with same-sex marriage, is that a good enough reason to support George Bush in all the pain and hardship he is causing in the world for no other reason than to serve the interests of the socioeconomic elites he aligns himself with? Is that a good enough reason to get with the neo-segregationist Jerry Falwell? So many of our folk get involved with or are fooled into supporting political conservatives whose policies are the antithesis of the ministry of liberation that Jesus claimed as his own in his inaugural sermon. Unless we speak prophetically, unless we speak the truth, folks won't know the difference and will continue to support those who do not support them.

If we are going to follow the example of Jesus, we have a responsibility to be prophets and to be prophetic. The prophetic imperative is ours and we must live it out first. If we speak prophetically often enough and energetically enough, it's going to make a difference. The Religious Right proves that. They redefine all kinds of things. They've even got some Black pastors speaking against liberalism. I want to say to those pastors, "If it was not for liberals and liberalism, you'd still be fighting for the right to vote." I'm not referring to moral liberalism. I'm talking about political liberalism. But the Religious Right redefines liberalism in such a way that now to be liberal is to be morally lax and maybe even unpatriotic. Well, if the Religious Right can set definitions, why can't those of us who embrace the true radicality of the gospel do the same? But we have to do it through living out the prophetic imperative.

Thus, there are certain realities we have to acknowledge. One of those realities is that people in the African American church are bibliolaters. That means that we are Bible-centered to the point that we all but worship the Bible. I certainly grew up that way. I believed that there was no Bible but the King James. And even then, if it wasn't the red letter version, then for me it wasn't really the Bible.

Alone, this high veneration for the Bible is not really a problem. What is a problem is that with the veneration for the Bible also comes veneration for traditional interpretations of biblical meaning, even if those interpretations are harmful to us and our loved ones or just plain don't make good sense. Still, today many Christians are locked into interpretations that are wrongheaded, even oppressive. This is a reality and it is not going to change anytime soon. Therefore, preachers and teachers have to study deeply so we can understand the Bible in its own context, what we call contextualization. This includes the biblical languages. Then we can draw enlightening analogies and bring the scriptures to life for our people in a way that empowers and edifies them, rather than deluding or confusing them.

As an example of contextualization, let's use the subject of spousal abuse. We may know people who stayed in marriages until they were crushed in body and spirit, if not destroyed, because their pastor might have told them, "Sister, I know he's beating you every week, but the Bible says you should not divorce except in the case of adultery." As a result of their pastor's uninformed interpretations, folks have stayed in these painful, even dangerous situations, thinking it was God's will for them to do so.

Now, contextualizing divorce—looking at its meaning in Jesus' time—tells us that in that era only men had the right to initiate marriage and to initiate divorce. So when Jesus spoke about divorce, he was talking only to men. And why was he speaking about divorce to men? Because, although divorce was a biblical prescription, abuse of it had distorted it into something other what than God had intended, and the use of it to mistreat women had become a widespread social phenomenon. Men used it to throw women aside and dispossess then at the husband's whim. So when Jesus spoke about divorce, he was indicting men for their abuse of it. He was telling them to stop it. He wasn't speaking to all situations for all time. He was speaking to a particular situation, to the abuse of divorce in his own time, when women had no rights at all. Things are different now, however. Now women have social and legal rights and protections. So when we contextualize Jesus' pronouncement about divorce, for instance, we see that it still applies to us, but it applies to us differently than it did in his time, because the historical situation is not the same. This is the importance of contextualizing, of taking into account the social and political context of the Bible.

As we seek to live out our prophetic call, it is important that we reclaim a tradition of interiority, of going silently inward to hear the voice of God. This is something that seems to seldom be done in churches anymore. In fact, if we have moments of meditation in the church at all, it's only for the few minutes at the end of the service while the choir recesses. Otherwise, there is no real time of meditation in our service where we sit in silence and experience the presence of God.

Reclaiming the tradition of interiority should not be done at the expense of studying the Bible, however, because the Bible is our standard, our guide. We cannot substitute personal, non-verifiable revelations and realizations for those of the Bible. But our study must be grounded in and informed by an interior, silent experience with God.

Finally, as we enact the prophetic imperative in our ministries, we need to reclaim pre-Constantinian Christianity. Before Emperor Constantine declared himself a Christian in 313 CE, Christianity was the faith of the oppressed. With Constantine's embrace of Christianity, however, it became the official religion of the oppressor. And in some way, shape, or form since that time, mainstream, post-Constantinian Christianity has been in league with those who are in control, with those who are the dominant elite in society. To maintain their privilege and control, dominant elites throughout history have had to flatten and distort every aspect of the gospel that empowers people to stand against exploitation and oppression. Otherwise, the prophetic power of the gospel would surely challenge their control.

The purpose of the prophetic imperative—as exemplified by prophets like Jeremiah, Isaiah, Ezekiel, Micah, Amos, culminating in Jesus—is to reclaim Christianity from the oppressive legacy of Constantine, to redirect the gaze of the Church to the time before principalities and powers took control of it and in the name of Christ started torturing and killing those who stood up for the true gospel of Christ. It is our calling to reclaim that Christianity. That is our imperative. That is our mandate. That is our sacred duty to God.

8.

Freeing the Captives

The Imperative of Womanist Theology

Jacquelyn Grant

As we consider the call to sound the trumpet in Zion so the captives will be free, we must evaluate the role of patriarchy in the Black church, the effects the Black church has on women, and the role of sex, lies, and violence in the very institution that preaches against the same. We must ask ourselves: Is the Black church detrimental for Black women's physical and psychological health? I am not a psychologist, nor a health or medical professional. I am simply a theologian trying to make some sense out of the waves of the church and their impact upon women in general, and Black women in particular. Perhaps it is my intention to raise more questions than to provide answers as we explore the challenges of a liberation.

Some form of the question "Is the church good for women's health?" came from a talk I heard given by Dr. Beverly Wildung Harrison, a retired ethics professor from Union Theological Seminary in New York. In the mid- to late 1970s, Dr. Harrison drew attention to the assault that women experienced in the church, historically and contemporarily. The same question is relevant in the Black church context. The question, of course, assumes or suggests that there may be something about the church that is in fact unhealthy for Black women. Those who take seriously the call to set the captives free should ask some more critical and poignant questions, such as: What do women find when they enter the church? What are women taught about themselves? about others? What are women taught about men in the church? What options does the church provide for women? How much of what happens to women inside and outside of the church is related to what the church teaches about women?

When I think about these and other related questions, my mind seems to focus on three things—sex, lies, and violence. Yes, I'm talking about the church, the place where we repeat the refrain: God is good all the time, and all the time God is good. Well, some may ask, if God is so good, why am I in so much pain when I go to church and try to do the right thing? If God is so good, then why is my life in such disorder? If God is so good, why does there appear to be more chaos than community—even in the church? Sex, lies, and violence seem to be matters to be condemned in the world, not in the church. Sometimes it does appear that the world is so much in the church. Sometimes it does appear that that which we preach against is often that which we live.

First, let's talk about sex in the church. Regina Taylor's depiction of women in the popular musical adaption of the book *Crowns*, written by Michael Cunningham and Craig Marberry,[1] presents what I consider an accurate portrayal of attitudes toward women as sexual temptress in the Black church. One of a variety of Black church customs highlighted in the play was the tradition of women covering their legs by pushing a sufficiently large handkerchief over their laps to hang below the knees when sitting in the front row. As this scene was being described, the voice quickly bellowed out the necessity of doing this in order to protect the pulpit from what was described as "the gates of hell or the gates to hell." This scene was probably the climax of the humor in the play, for—in the lingo of the theater—it brought down the house.

As the crowd bellowed with laughter, I thought, "Isn't it interesting how we have bought into the distortions about women?" We have bought into the notion that women have been and still are the cause of men's sexual perversities. It brought to mind what church fathers have said about women. In the third century Tertullian wrote that women are the devil's gateway. He addressed women, asking, Do you not know that you are each an Eve? The sentence of God on this sex of yours lives in this age. The guilt must of necessity live, too. You are the devil's gateway. You are the unsealer of that forbidden tree. You are the first deserter of the divine law. You are she who persuaded him who the devil was not valiant enough to attack on account of your dessert—that is death. Even the Son of God had to die.[2]

Well, Tertullian was not by himself in that kind of thinking. Salimbene of Adam, a thirteenth-century Franciscan monk, wrote that woman was "evil from the beginnings, a gate of death, a disciple of the servant, the devil's accomplice, a fount of deception, a dogstar to godly labors, rust corrupting the saints; whose perilous face hath overthrown such as had already become almost angels. Lo, woman is the head of sin—a weapon of the devil, expulsion from Paradise, mother of guilt, corruption of the ancient law."

And good ole Saint Augustine said: What is the difference whether it is in a wife or a mother, it is still Eve—the tempest that we must be aware of in any woman. I fail to see what use women can be to men if one excludes the function of bearing children.[3]

Interestingly, I've never heard of men's genitalia being referred to as the devil's staff or men's forceful hand being compared to Satan's tools. I've never heard of men's offices being referred to as Satan's workshops.

During my candidacy for ministry, one of my pastoral counseling teachers spent almost the entire period discussing how ministers can steer clear of those "you-know-what"—women. The same teacher had nothing to offer when I asked what women should do when invitations to preach turned into propositions, or when counseling sessions turned into invitations to help the woman preacher by giving her the good sex that would solve all of her problems.

Unfortunately, the matter of sex in the church could be discussed at length, but let's move on to lies.

In his book, *Ten Lies the Church Tells Women*,[4] J. Lee Grady lists some of the common ones in today's church. Grady says that the first lie is that God created women as inferior beings designed to serve their husbands. The second lie is that women are not equipped to assume leadership roles in the church. The third lie is that women must not teach or preach to men in a church setting. The fourth lie is that a woman should view her husband as the priest of the home. Number five is that a man needs to cover a woman in her ministry activities. Lie number six says that women who exhibit strong leadership qualities pose a serious danger to the church. Lie number seven says women are more easily deceived than men. Lie number eight says women cannot be fulfilled or spiritually effective without a husband and children. Lie number nine says women shouldn't work outside of the home. And lie number ten says that women must obediently submit to their husbands in all situations.

Grady talks about how the Bible has been misused to keep women in spiritual bondage. Using much of what has already been revealed and researched by revisionists, reformists, and feminists about biblical interpretation in recent years, Grady, a white evangelical male, however, proceeds to bash feminist accomplishments in the last three decades.[5] He uses their work, but his evangelical groundedness prevents him from giving credit where credit is due. In spite of his theological and moral shortcomings, Grady does identify some of the biblical areas that provide reasons for women's great concerns.

It is true that the church has been guilty of putting women in various kinds of prisons. In my work, I've talked about one prison called sexism. Women must be silent in the church—except if we need a choir or a soloist or someone to read the announcements and welcome the visitors. As a woman, your place is in the home—except when you're needed to take care of the chores to keep the church running. Women may not pastor—unless they are needed for those small and sometime rural churches that men do not care for. You may not minister because you bring too much baggage with you.

If a female minister has a husband, the church asks, What does he think about your being in ministry? Now, there isn't really anything wrong with the question. It is good and quite appropriate that the church is concerned about the impact of the itinerant ministry on the family of the minister. The problem is in the fact that there seems to be no concern for the feelings and thoughts of the wife in the case of a male minister.

And if the female pastor does not have a husband, there must be something wrong with her. Homophobia is made manifest. "You must be a lesbian"—as if that is the worst thing you can be. One pastor said to a lesbian, "All you need is a good man, and I'm that man." Of course, he didn't say what his wife thought about the idea.

And, finally, let's look at violence in the church. In his work as a program manager at Men Stopping Violence in Atlanta, Sulaiman Nuriddin works with men sent to him by the court system; these men are required to be involved in counseling and/or support-group work, or they will be jailed for domestic violence convictions. He said a surprisingly large number of men attend the support-group sessions with their Bibles in hand, reciting the passage "Wives be submissive to your husbands" (in the NRSV, "Wives . . . accept the authority of your husbands," 1 Peter 3:1). These men seem to think that the Bible mandates submission for women in relation to men and that if necessary, women must be beaten into submission. We see again and again that there is a history of this badgering of the Bible, which results in the battering of women. One husband said, "Take up a stick and beat her—not in rage, but out of charity and concern for her soul so that the beating will rebound to your credit and to her good."

Well, good brother Martin Luther said, "Women must neither begin nor complete anything without a man."[6] Where he is, there she must be and bend before him as before a master, whom she shall fear and to whom she shall be subject and obedient.

Well, Susan Thistlewaite reminds us that women with a violent spouse have believed that the Bible actually says what they have been taught it says. They believe that women are inferior in status before husband and God and deserve a life of pain.

James Alsdurf conducted a study on the matter of domestic violence and how the church deals with it, and these are some of the findings he published:[7] Twenty-six percent of pastors polled said that they normally tell a woman who is being abused by her husband that she should continue to submit to him and to trust that God will honor her action by either stopping the abuse or giving her the strength to endure. About 25 percent of the respondents said a lack of submissiveness in the wife is what triggered the violence in the first place. In other words, these pastors believe that the abuse is actually the woman's fault. The women are told that if they would learn to submit, the violence would stop. The majority of the pastors said it is better for a woman to tolerate some level of violence in the home—even though it is not God's perfect will—than to seek separation that might end in divorce. They said this tolerance is better even if the woman is killed, maimed, or raped. Seventy-one percent of the ministers said that they would never advise a battered wife to leave her husband or separate because of abuse, and 92 percent said they would never counsel her to seek divorce.

As I conclude, based on the beliefs of many misguided clerics, being in the church can really be dangerous to the health of women. And in some instances it can even be life-threatening. How do we reconcile all of these unhealthy activities in the church with the other side of the church's story—that story that we like to tell and tell over and over again? For it is in the church where we find Black women who are able to move from victim to vessel—to use the words of A. Elaine Crawford.[8] We can celebrate the achievements of women who were able to find strength in spite of the oppressive structures of the church. We can celebrate the work of these women who were able to look beyond the sins of the church and to find salvation. We can celebrate the work of women who were able to redeem the church as they sought redemption for themselves. We can celebrate women like Jarena Lee, who was able to see Christ as a whole Savior instead of half of one, as many would have us believe. We indeed can celebrate that we can say with loud voices, as we are reminded by Cheryl Townsend Gilkes, in the vernacular of the people in spite of the sins of the church: "If it wasn't for the women . . ."—now, you finish the statement.

9.

The Biblical Basis for a Political Theology of Liberation

Randall C. Bailey

As I REFLECT ON HOW WE CAN LEARN from our ancestors to continue a political theology of liberation, I begin with a personal story as a scholar and church person to locate myself socially. One evening when I arrived at home from teaching a late class, my son, Omari, called me into the den. He was around eleven years old at the time, and he was watching the movie *The King of Kings*. He said, "Look, Dad, that's Pontius Pilate, that's Jesus, and that's Barabbas. Watch and see; they're going to choose Barabbas."

And the crowd in the movie did choose to set Barabbas free instead of Jesus of Nazareth. Omari was proud of what he was learning in church school. The next thing the movie depicted was the crucifixion. The camera went back and forth from Jesus to the crowd. When the camera landed on Jesus, he would say something; then the camera would pan out to the crowd. Each time the camera would show Jesus, an amazed Omari would say: "I can hear him."

I said, "Yes, those are words recorded in the Gospels that Jesus was supposed to have uttered from the cross."

My son then replied, "But in school we sang, 'They crucified my savior and he never said a mumbling word.' Now, I can hear him speaking from the cross."

This interaction with my son, who has some very profound theological questions but who has not yet joined the church in twenty-seven years, set me on the path to exploring the disjunction to which he pointed. It seems that in this particular spiritual our people rewrote the story of the crucifixion. I'm sure they were aware of the tradition of the seven last words, but they chose not to follow that tradition in telling the story. Instead, to retell the story of Christ our ancestors turned to the tradition of African martyrdom, in which the martyr does not speak at the lynching—for to do so would be to dignify the lynching. This is why revolt leader Nat Turner didn't speak at his trial, and that's why our ancestors depicted Jesus as an African martyr in their spiritual. They sang, "They crucified my savior and [just like an African martyr] he never said a mumbling word."

Our ancestors felt that it was perfectly alright to change the story to be in line with our religious experience and understanding. Sometimes they kept to the story, as with "Go Down, Moses." At other times they altered the story by connecting the Hebrew Bible story with the New Testament story, as in "We Are Climbing Jacob's Ladder." The song says, "We are climbing Jacob's ladder . . . for we are soldiers of the cross." While the Hebrew Bible's account of Jacob's ladder says it extended to heaven and was lined with angels, our foreparents said that when you climb that ladder, you've got to go through the cross.

Our ancestors thought that it was perfectly alright to change the story to fit their religious experience. To further explain this methodology, I use the example of the spiritual "Oh Mary, Oh Martha, Don't You Weep, Don't You Moan" in my article "The Danger of Ignoring One's Own Cultural Bias in Interpreting the Text."[1] The spiritual refers to the pericope in John 11 when Lazarus dies before Jesus arrives; Mary and Martha yell angrily at Jesus, saying that he should have shown up before their brother died. After Jesus cries and proclaims that he is the life and the resurrection, he calls Lazarus to come forth from the tomb.

Our foreparents, who lived their lives on the plantation during their enslavement, saw their Lazaruses sexually abused, sold off to other plantations, whipped, castrated, raped, and sometimes killed. Jesus wasn't showing up in time to stop their Lazaruses' tragedies and deaths, nor were their Lazaruses returning from their graves. Since our ancestors' religious experience did not conform to the biblical story, they rewrote the story in the spiritual; they told Mary and Martha not to weep and not to moan—not because Jesus was the life and the resurrection, but because Pharaoh's army got drowned. The promise that the white enslavers like the Egyptian Pharaoh would be killed is what gave them the eschatological hope that they could live through slavery. In this instance, instead of relying on the salvific message of Jesus, resurrection and life, our ancestors found their story in the salvific message of Yahweh delivering the Israelites from Pharaoh's army. Our foreparents taught us that it is alright to change the story to be in line with our religious experience. The notions of a fundamentalist reading of the biblical text were foreign to what our people understood as the way to read the Bible.

The story of Howard Thurman's grandmother teaches us the same lesson. Thurman's grandmother had been enslaved and used to hear the slave preachers preach under an injunction from Ephesians 6: "Slaves, obey your earthly masters" (v. 5). Because of the slave owners' sermons, grandmother threw Paul out of the Bible and wouldn't let Thurman read to her from any of the Pauline text, with the exception of the love chapter, 1 Corinthians 13. In other words, Thurman's grandmother was teaching that if the text sanctions oppression in our religious experience, such a text is not spiritual. It may be in the Bible, but it is not spiritual.

I'm not advocating a strategy of throwing these texts out, because I think we need to engage these texts; we need to struggle with them and struggle against them, an option used by many Black people. But it seems that some of us have broken from our religious tradition and heritage in the ways in which we read the Bible and in the authority we ascribe to the Bible.

What does rereading the text in context with our story have to do with social justice? I contend that part of the problem in our addressing social justice issues in the church is this fundamentalist claim on the text, which prohibits us from reading the text through our own stories and prevents us from recognizing when the text itself is steering us away from social justice.

The text provides several illustrations of Jesus as a king who claims royal power and a following among the people and, therefore, a political threat to the Roman state. To clearly understand Christ as king, we need to understand the Hebrew Bible context of kings. In 2 Samuel 7, we have the story of David wanting to build the temple. The Lord said that David should not build the temple but that his son would build it. Then the Lord establishes David's throne forever. "He shall build a house for my name, and I will establish the throne of his kingdom forever. I will be a father to him, and he shall be a son to me" (vv. 13-14). From this text we see that the king of Judah was known as the son of God.

At the point of coronation, the king became the son of God by adoption, according to Ps. 2:6-7: "I have set my king on Zion, my holy hill. I will tell of the decree of the Lord: He said to me, 'You are my son; today, I have begotten you.'" By the same token, in 1 Samuel 24–26 we see instances when David could have killed Saul, the king of Israel. Yet David says, "Touch not the Lord's anointed—the Messiah" (based on 1 Chron. 16:22; Ps. 105:15). The Greeks translate Messiah into *Christos*, the Christ. So, according to the Hebrew and Greek text, the Messiah, the Christos, the Christ is a translation of the anointed one, which is another term for the king.

In Mark 1:1 we read the beginning of the good news of Jesus Christos—the Son of God. Jesus is called Christos, or Messiah, or anointed one. And Jesus is called Son of God, which means king. Jesus is understood to be a king or at least a kingly figure. Therefore, Jesus should be understood as having political intentions. According to the Gospel of Mark, he is a king, a political king. We miss this, on the one hand, because we don't connect the terms with their Hebrew Bible context. We also miss the kingship of Christ because we read the story through Luke's and Matthew's virgin birth narratives, although both Gospels trace Jesus to the lineage of David. However, Jesus has been so spiritualized by Paul that even when the text presents him as Son of God, as Christ, as the king, we miss it, or even worse we reject it.

In Amos 4, Amos tells the rich of Samaria, whom he calls the oppressor, "They should take you away with hooks, even the last of you with fish hooks" (v. 2). In this passage fishing is used as a metaphor for destruction of the oppressor. This metaphor is also used in the same way in Jeremiah and Ezekiel. Brian Blount, professor of New Testament at Princeton Theological Seminary, in his book *Go Preach!* argues that in Jesus' invitation to discipleship—follow me and become fishers of humans—Jesus moves this metaphor out of the oppressive/destruction category to an evangelism motif.[2] But what if Blount and the rest of the traditional readings of this so-called discipleship are wrong? What if Jesus is in line with Hebrew Bible prophetic tradition? If so, "follow me to become fishers of men and women" would be a call to join a revolutionary band that would get rid of the Romans and the Herodians and reestablish justice and righteousness. But we are used to ignoring political language in the text, and we don't want Jesus to be political because that might mean we have to be political.

So Jesus' triumphant entrance into Jerusalem is a reenactment of the liturgy in which the king comes to the temple in Jerusalem during a time of war, when the enemy has initially been defeated but the war isn't over yet; the people still need the Lord's help. Then the priest says, "Blessed is the one who comes in the name of the Lord," and they instruct the people to place branches on the ground for the king to pass over on the way to the altar. In the entry into Jerusalem, the priests are plotting against Jesus. So the people take over the priestly function, and they proclaim, "Hosanna, save us. Blessed is the one who comes in the name of the Lord." The good news about the people's action in place of the priest is that when clergy do not act right, the laity can act right in spite of us.

Another illustration of Jesus' political mission is the crucifixion. The Romans used crucifixion as a public lynching for runaway slaves, political revolutionaries, and traitors to the Roman state. Crucifixions were public events to keep a colonized people in line, to stop slavery boasting, and to ensure obedience by Roman citizens. Now, since Jesus was crucified, in what category do you want to put him? He was not a Roman citizen, so he could not have been a traitor to the Roman state; he was not depicted as a slave; so this would mean that Jesus was a political revolutionary. With all of this talk of "Son of God," Peter's confession of Christ as the anointed one or the king, and Jesus' triumphal and kingly entry into Jerusalem, the text unmistakably depicts Jesus as a king claiming royal power and a following among the people. He is therefore a political threat to the Roman state.

Another reason we miss Jesus as political revolutionary and threat to the Roman Empire is that the Gospels keep stressing the role of the Jews and minimizing the role of the Roman state for the cruci-fixion. Even at the Pentecost, Peter prays and talks about how the Jews killed him, which is an impossibility; the Jews could not perform capital punishment. But the writers of the text keep trying to shift the blame from the Roman state because they are writing to Theophilus, and they want to keep the Greeks and the Romans on their side. And then the writers start saying that Jesus died for our sins—our lying, cheating, stealing, smoking, cursing, having sex—as opposed to dying because he was empowering the people to fight against their oppres-sion and to pick up their own cross. However, if we think that picking up the cross means empowered to fight oppression, then we can't say that my cross is my inability to lose weight, my drug-head child, my spouse with Alzheimer's. Under this model we cannot continue to make our personal problems a cross. We see the cross as a revolution-ary call to fight against oppression and unite the people to understand that when we deal with drugs, we have to deal with individual addic-tion, but we also have an obligation to close down crack houses. The revolutionary cross will put you in the line of fire.

The Last Supper is figured to take place on the Passover. This is a holiday celebrating the liberation from Egypt. Could this not also mean that communion is tied to the liberation struggles of our people? When Jesus says, "Do this in remembrance of me," is he saying, "Pass out crackers and grape juice," or is he saying, "Do the type of liberating things that I did in the community"? Feed the five thousand out of your own resources instead of through a faith-based handout from the government. The real miracle in this context was getting the church to fund the feeding program itself. Make medical services free to the people as Jesus did in healing the lepers—that was the first Medicaid program. We have to teach the congregations that the communion is a covenant ceremony: we come to the table and we promise God that we shall carry forth the liberation activities of Jesus in our community. Unfortunately, we have over-spiritualized Jesus, which means that we can stay spiritual and stay above all of the problems in our community.

The Ethiopian official who requests baptism in Acts 8 is convinced of the faith because of its connection with the theology of a suffering servant and its connection to seeking justice. What would happen if our rituals of baptism were made explicit as acts of initiation into a revolutionary religion seeking the well-being of all, bringing life and making life more abundant in the community? As we are baptized into this revolutionary band, we understand that taking drugs is counterrevolutionary. I told my son that I stopped smoking pot in college because I was missing too many Civil Rights marches—I was too high to go. My responsibility to the cause showed me that drugs were counterrevolutionary. As I recalled my story, I apologized to my son because my generation has not passed on the revolution that can move the next generation out of the state they are in.

We have to start looking at using communion, using baptism, as a way of calling us forth to "do this in remembrance of me." Do the liberation activities in memory of Christ. Bring Christ alive in ways that show us that you may get killed, you may even be fired, you may not even be invited back, but God has another word for you on the other side of what's done to you. Nothing that this society can do for you is ultimate. Only what God will do for you is ultimate. If you dare, do the just thing and get crucified—you will be resurrected!

10.

And the Bible Says

Methodological Tyranny of Biblical Fundamentalism and Historical Criticism

Delman L. Coates

As a scholar and historian of early Christianity, I have observed that there are some particular presuppositions and approaches to the biblical text that impede the Black Churches' and the Black pastor's ability to be prophetic. These presuppositions and approaches hinder the kind of prophetic, hermeneutical, and theological imaginations needed to liberate the captives. I would like to deal with the theoretical and methodological obstacles of contemporary interpretive practice that prevent us from achieving the kind of broad reflective reading and application of the biblical text that we need.

Whether we are practitioners, preachers, or professional academicians in the contemporary world, the reading of the Bible is hampered by our historical relationship to three historical moments. The first is the Protestant Reformation of the sixteenth century. The second is the Scientific Revolution that swept Europe in the late sixteenth and seventeenth centuries, and the third is the Enlightenment (late seventeenth to eighteenth centuries). These three decisive cultural and intellectual movements are important because they have contributed to presupposition and epistemological categories that we bring to the task of biblical interpretation.

Because we are on this side of those three moments, we tend to assume that the ultimate truth of the Bible is based upon whether our reading of the text conforms to several categories—objectivity, historicity, and scientific positivism—and, therefore, one literal meaning.

The problem with this current interpretive situation, which I view as a crisis, is that it obscures the fact that the world that produced the writings we call sacred was not a product of modernity. Modernity has produced two methodological offspring that, I think, impede our ability to develop the kind of spiritual understanding and biblical practice needed for a liberation theology. These two children are biblical fundamentalism and the historical-critical study of the Bible and of early Christianity.

First, let's consider biblical fundamentalism. It is important for us to know that fundamentalism—with its attending rhetoric about the literal inerrant historical objective and scientific character of the biblical narrative—was a reaction to the emerging scientific view of the world, which fundamentalists saw as a threat to biblical faith. In order to respond to the challenges posed by the scientific and philosophical communities, Christian fundamentalists conformed biblical meaning to the same scientific categories being set forward by these "secularists," for lack of a better word.

Despite its rhetoric—that is, that of being the only true approach to reading the biblical text—fundamentalism is really a secular discourse and is foreign to classical varieties of early Christian and Protestant understandings of scriptural truth. In the past fifty years, with an increase in African American literacy, education, and social standing, the fundamentalist mentality has become increasingly influential among us. It is important for those of us who teach, preach, and are inspired by scripture to understand that biblical fundamentalism is a racial class discourse that uses the Bible to smuggle and camouflage social and political agendas underneath our noses.

Fundamentalism should be of concern for us for the reasons just mentioned, but also because biblical fundamentalism runs concurrent with the denial of social and political opportunities for Black people in America. That is, whenever Blacks sought freedom in this country, the twisted notions about fundamental biblical truth were used to try to suppress our liberation. The Bible should never be used to prevent intellectual and spiritual engagement with the text in light of our contemporary needs and realities.

With many of us sympathetic to or trained in Western theological schools and opposed to the fundamentalist approach we have been accustomed to, historical-critical methodology—while invaluable in many respects—is no less a problematic interpretive discourse.

I am concerned about our embrace of European (German) reconstructions of early Christianity, in particular certain versions of the historical Jesus created to advance particular social and political ends.

Historical criticism is not a disinterested historical inquiry that is free from ideological interests and presuppositions. Historical criticism—like the fundamentalist worldview—presents itself as an agenda-less discourse, but it has really emerged instead as a theoretical tool to advance European (colonial) agendas.

So how do we begin dealing with the situation presented by these two discourses? What we need is an alternative biblical practice that is rooted in an alternative epistemological framework. To do this, however, requires that we develop a greater awareness of the histories of these two interpretive discourses.

What is needed is a greater knowledge of the history of the categories, presuppositions, and methods we have inherited, or else we stand in jeopardy of pouring old European and German hermeneutical wine into new African wineskins, and this will not work. Both historical criticism and biblical fundamentalism are guided by particular ideological presuppositions and cultural interests that are not in the interest of the people we serve. They also subordinate the Bible to categories of which the people who wrote, read, and heard them were not aware.

The purpose of considering the historical development of the field is to disclose the ideological interests that have shaped and determined the traditional critical approaches to the study of the Bible. In my mind an alternative African spiritual practice of the Bible requires that we expose dominant cultural ideologies that have shaped biblical fundamentalism and evangelical Christianity as well as so-called liberal Protestant historical-critical methodologies.

New methodological terrain means that we have to decenter these frameworks in order to center the critical interpretive task upon the spiritual, experiential, and social world of African and African American people. An African American biblical hermeneutic—and I want to say this to challenge us—is more than just taking the characters of the Bible and painting them Black. That is important, but a critical African discourse has to move beyond it.

In conclusion, let me remind you that as election years approach, the Religious Right always uses wedge issues in order to appeal to our people. We cannot be distracted by the attention to these wedge issues that, according to what Ralph Reed said in 1988, the Right needs to use in order to get Black people's support. Today's wedge issues are abortion, gay marriage, and so forth. Although those are serious issues, they often take the spotlight off of health care, the AIDS epidemic in Africa, jobs being exported abroad, and so on.

As we consider developing a biblical framework for Africans and African Americans, I want to recommend three things: Shawn Kelly's book *Racializing Jesus*—I would encourage you read it; the book discusses some challenges that have been addressed at this conference.[1] I also want to encourage participation by more preachers in the Society of Biblical Literature and the American Academy of Religion. It is important for preachers to be a part of this larger discourse. And, third, let me say that as the Samuel DeWitt Proctor Conference continues to evolve, I would caution against the development of numerous separate groups. For me it runs the risk of compartmentalizing the great collection of preachers and scholars gathered here and would result in the participants' retreating to our own ideological neighborhoods with preachers on one side and scholars on the other, with those interested in social justice here and those interested in growing their churches over there. I would encourage a continued synthetic experience in order to bring about liberation to all groups.

III

The Sermon as Deed

11.

The Priestly Faithful and Prophetically Courageous

Charles G. Adams

THOSE CALLED BY GOD to proclaim the good news need to be both faithful and courageous. Our prophetical call, however, does not come without a cost. Managing the enmity of foes and friends requires a teachable spirit and contentment with failure. We are not usually in a very teachable mood until life has whipped us into an attitude to learn and a willingness to change; then God can get our undivided attention.

How many beatings will we have to take before we are teachable enough to realize that no matter what is going on in us or around us, God is with us and not against us? Paul's exhortation in Rom. 8:31-39 reminds us of God's attributes—supremely able with absolute power and unconditional love. This text is radical. It is bold and audacious, and it seems unreasonable, imponderable, and unbelievable. What does Paul mean—no one is against us, or no one or nothing can be against us? This great apostle to the nations declares this to us in our teachable moment, when the world seems to be falling apart and there is trouble everywhere.

The world is in conflict. The whole economy of the world is going down. The world is threatened by terrorism. Jobs are disappearing, and there is more war than peace, more poverty than plenty, more grief than joy, more sickness than health, more uncertainty than security, more violence than safety, serenity, or sanity. So what does Paul mean by "no one can be against us"? This doesn't make sense. In this world there are many problems to be solved, and we don't know where to begin. High-handed sin is out there. It needs to be corrected, and yet we don't have enough repentance.

There are enemies who need to be redeemed and restored, and we don't have enough love in our hearts to reach out to them. So, how are we to believe—much less learn—that no one is against and no one can be against us?

Look at the poverty rate and the imbalance of wealth in this world. Absolute poverty is defined as the lack of sufficient income in cash or in kind to meet the most basic biological needs for food, clothing, and shelter. Absolute poverty is the principle cause of human misery and death in the world today. Absolutely poor people consume an average of 180 kilos of grain a year, while Europeans and North Americans average 900 kilos of grain a year.

Only by transferring some of the wealth of rich nations to poor nations can the situations that are so deplorable around the world be changed. We, however, are so committed to our luxuries that it does not bother us that the rest of the world does not have necessities and that very little is being transferred to the poorer nations. The United Nations say that 0.7 percent of any nation's gross national product (GNP) should be given to the underdeveloped afflicted nations of the world. Compare that number to the 0.5 percent spent on alcohol and the 0.3 percent spent on tobacco. Not only does the United Nations say that we should give 0.7 percent as a nation, but as voluntary associations we should chip in another small percentage, and then the other nations would have what they need. Well, here's the record of giving: Germany gives 0.41 percent. Japan gives 0.23 percent. Britain gives 0.63 percent. And the United States, the richest nation in the world, gives 0.15 percent of its gross national product—fifteen cents out of every one hundred dollars.[1] One might reasonably say that we are all murderers if we permit our affluence to cause billions of hungry people to die because we are not as knowledgeable as we could be, not as sensitive as we should be, or not as involved as we would be if we took time out to thank God for all God had done for us and share with others. The duty to avoid killing is much easier to discharge than the duty to save human lives—actively and aggressively in the moral sense of the term.[2]

However, in this lyrical and theologically celebrated song in Rom. 8:31-39, there is little mention of anything that is negative at all. Paul asks, "If God is for us, who is against us?" (v. 31). Paul's answer is "no one," but he doesn't explain it. To find more of an exploration of the negative aspects of life, you have to go to other Pauline scriptures; even then, whenever Paul mentions anything negative, he does so dismissively and not exhaustively. In 2 Cor. 6:3-5, Paul lets us know that he is not in denial of evil and trouble in the world. He says to those who feel that somehow or other he is not qualified to be a preacher because he didn't go to the school they went to, or because he was not an eyewitness to Jesus Christ, or because he didn't dress like a preacher, that he is not making anything an obstacle to anyone's faith. He says, "I want no fault to be found with my ministry." As servants of God, like Paul, we have commended ourselves in every way through great endurances—through afflictions and hardships and calamities and beatings and imprisonment and riots and labors and sleepless nights and hunger. Paul does not ignore all of the ills of his own soul, nor does he deny the troubles and injustices of the world.

In 2 Cor. 12:7 Paul says that he had a rendezvous with God face-to-face in the third heaven. Paul said he couldn't even describe them—the great revelations that he had in the third heaven. But when he came back to earth, Satan was waiting for him at the foot of the ladder with a thorn to plant in Paul's flesh. The thorn was a messenger of Satan to buffet him, to keep him from becoming too elated over the revelations that he had seen. When you are really serving God and when you're really feeling good, you've got to look out because Satan will send a messenger. When you think you are closest to God, Satan will send a strange messenger.

So, Paul says, I've got a thorn in the flesh, and I prayed three times that God would take it out. I know that some folks say, "Just name it and claim it," but Paul named it and he couldn't claim it. The thorn still stayed in his flesh. But one day in the midnight hour, Jesus told him: "I'm not going to take it out. I can do more for you than take it out. I can show you something that you can't see until you suffer. I'm going to let it stay there so I can bless you by it and develop you in it and prosper you with it and strengthen you for it and encourage you through it, because my grace is sufficient for you."

God didn't take Paul's thorn away, and God will not take ours away. That particular thorn will never be removed on this side of the grave. With all of this in mind, it does not sound like Paul is one to deny the reality of suffering, sin, pain, and death in the world and especially in the ministry.

We should take note from Paul. Do not expect that everyone in your middle-class church will welcome a message of liberation and a prophetic gospel. Some of the members in these high-class Black churches have cut their own deals and have their own connections with people in power. They don't want your preaching to mess with their arrangements. They'll call a meeting on you, and you'll think that you don't have a friend in the world. But I want you to know, Paul said, that when those times come to you, God's grace is still sufficient. And if God is for you—even when you fail—nobody can be against you. Sometimes this is the cost for being the priestly faithful and prophetically courageous.

Dr. Peter Gomes, Plummer Professor of Christian Morals and Pusey Minister in the Memorial Church at Harvard University, tells Harvard seniors that if they are not acquainted with failure and how to deal with it, then they are not prepared for life and how to live it. So it is necessary for all of us to come to terms with failure because failure more than success will define our lives. You will learn not so much how to market success as to cope successfully with failure. Sometimes you succeed in business and fail in family. Sometimes you can succeed in getting money and lose the contentment and peace of your heart and mind. Sometimes you can get what you want and then turn around and not want what you got. Sometimes failure will grab you in the midst of your success. Can you deal successfully with failure? Perhaps there's no other success than knowing how to cope successfully with failure.

What are you going to do when you don't get the job you are qualified for? when they don't give you tenure? when those who are far less qualified than you go clambering up the greasy pole to the top while you are left standing, looking up? when your best friends turn against you? when your stocks lose all their value? Gomes says that the test of a person is not on the mountaintop of success but in the deep valley of defeat, where most ordinary people must spend most of their time.[3]

What are you going to do when trouble and treachery and tragedy are so tough and so obvious that they cannot and will not be ignored or denied? The point is not to deny failure, but to work in failure and through failure and despite failure until we have turned failure into the success that comes to us by learning that God is still with us—even in failure. God never left us, and we cannot go from God's presence. When you put your trust in God, you will discover that God has already put more trust in you than you are able to put in God. God believes in you more than you believe in God or yourself. It is only by failure that we have learned how minute, temporary, transitory, and weak failure really is in comparison to the presence, purpose, power, and glory of our God. Failure is real, but God is more real. Failure is tough, but God is more powerful. And God will give you strength to turn failure into a successful spiritual life.

One of these days you're going to learn how to thank God for your burdens. For if you never had a problem, you wouldn't know God could solve them. I've learned that if God is for you, nobody can be against you. Not even death can be against you.

Our heroes of faith—many of whom we honor at this conference—have also learned this lesson. Look at Samuel Proctor, Prathia Hall, Miles Jerome Jones, Jeremiah A. Wright Sr., Charles B. Coffer, Frederick George Sampson, E. K. Bailey Jr., Anthony C. Campbell, James Coston, and others who now rest from their labor. Let them tell you, "Keep on doing what you're doing. Keep on preaching the prophetically courageous word. If God is for you, nobody can be against you, because God can take bad things and make them your friends. Even your mistakes will become your major professors. When your enemies turn against you and become your emissaries, they will make you more famous than you would have been if you didn't have somebody talking about you." Joseph said to his enemy brothers, "Even though you intended to do harm to me, God intended it for good" (Gen. 50:20). For if God is for you, nobody can be against you.

In our focal text, Paul was testifying to a faith that had been forged in failure. He said, "I've had plenty of trouble to deal with, but God took my failure and forged it into fortitude." Look how we as an African people have been forged in the fires of persecution and failure. If it had been left to the enemy, we would have been dead a long time ago. We would have all drowned in the North Atlantic or perished in the Middle Passage. But look what God has done through many afflictions, hardships, and calamities, beatings and sleepless nights and hungry days.

God kept you alive, kept your hands in the hands of Jesus. God has brought us through, and we're able to rejoice. And nobody can be against us. Even when we want to be against us, we cannot be against ourselves. God will take every drawback and every hard hit and turn it into a blessing.

God uses every adversity as a teachable moment—to let us know that all things work together for good. All things will help you on your way because God believes in us more than we believe in God.

We have been saved by grace—not by our thoughts, not by our faith, not by our prayers. God has invested too much in us to let us be destroyed like trash or a pile of rubbish. We are God's own children, designed for God's glory. God has faith in us, and it will never fail. God has love for us, and it will never turn us loose. God has hope in us, and it will never be disappointed.

And look what we have from God: committed comfort, corrective chastisement, continuing challenge, certain change, constant contentment, and ceaseless celebration. If God be for us, who can be against us? We have hope in every situation. We have help in every generation. We have light in every midnight. We have victory in every calamity.

How shall God not also freely with Jesus give us all things? If he gives you Jesus, he'll also give you justice. If he gives you salvation, he'll also give you strength. If he gives you life, he'll also keep you alive until your work is done. If God is for you, you can be for God and for others. Who will bring any charge against God's elect? Who can accuse you when God has forgiven you? Who can run a guilt trip on you when God has said you're alright?

You are going to have trouble. If it's not slavery, it's segregation. If it's not segregation, it's discrimination. If it's not discrimination, it's intimidation. If it's not intimidation, it's investigation. If it's not investigation, it's prejudice. If it's not prejudice, it's powerlessness. If it's not powerlessness, it's unemployment. If it's not unemployment, it's hell on the job. If it's not Ronald Reagan, it's George H. W. Bush. If it's not George H. W. Bush, it's George W. Bush. If it's not Bush, it's nicotine. If it's not nicotine, it's morphine. If it's not morphine, it's alcohol. If it's not alcohol, it's crack cocaine. If it's not crack cocaine, it's calories and grease and salt and high blood pressure. Everybody's got a problem. But let me tell you something: if God is for you, nobody can be against you.

What battle can God not own? What sickness can God not heal? What shall separate us from the love of God? Shall hardship, distress, persecution, famine, nakedness, peril, sword, sickness, sorrow, pain, death? "In all these things we are more than conquerors through him that loved us" (Rom. 8:37). For I am persuaded; I'm absolutely certain; I'm totally convinced; I'm sure that neither death nor life, neither angels nor principalities, neither things present nor things to come, neither powers nor rulers, neither height nor death, nor any other creature will be able to separate us from the love of God which is in Christ Jesus.

12.

Running the Race for Future Generations

Can You Handle the Faith without the Fulfillment?

Renita J. Weems

As a Hebrew Bible scholar and preacher I reside in two homes—the academy and the church. These two are jealous, demanding lovers that insist upon my undivided attention and unswerving loyalty. They unrelentingly ask, "Which one will you be—a preacher or a scholar?"

I chose to concentrate on the Old Testament because one verse in Hebrews arrested my imagination and filled me with longing to know and to study more about God, religion, the Bible, faith, and the history of a people whose longings and journey was from a struggle, through a struggle, and to a struggle. I am taken by this writer's careful exegesis of the Old Testament scripture and Hebrew history. The writer of Hebrews explains what it means to be the people of the new covenant.

When this letter is written, it is the last third of the first century, when this church found itself struggling to survive amid a changing political, religious, and economic environment, frustrated with having to live with delayed promises. Delayed promises are the best way to describe and characterize a small Christian congregation that stands behind the book of Hebrews. Members of a small, persecuted congregation struggle to hold fast to their belief in a crucified Judean carpenter as the risen Savior, and are faced with the dissonance of living and worshiping in the midst of a largely half-Jewish/half-pagan, hostile society.

Years, perhaps decades, have passed since these people have heard the good news of the kingdom of God with all of its attendant promises. And now they must ask themselves, "Did I really hear right? Is this really the right path I'm supposed to be taking? Did I hear right about who Jesus Christ was?" And so in the midst of a hostile, half-pagan/half-Jewish culture, this Jewish Christian audience is now looking at maybe thirty years since the last time they heard from God—delayed promises.

These Christians live in a hostile environment, during the reign of Nero, an emperor who would eventually blame Christians as a scapegoat for a fire that he set in Rome. The Church is under persecution and under struggle, having to redefine itself. The church has to revisit some of the old promises to see if it had gotten it right. And so the people in the church probably have written this unknown writer of the book of Hebrews to ask, "Is it all in vain?"

Considerable differences of opinion over doctrine, theology, and church history have cropped up in the church, leaving the congregation dismayed, disheartened, and divided. Everybody is pulling in different directions and arguing over dogma and practices. Instead of having a social element to the ministry, instead of going out and preaching good news to the captives and setting the oppressed free, the church is arguing over the exegesis of the book of Genesis, whether homosexuals really ought to belong to the church, and should we have more women bishops? The Christians are quibbling over doctrine, while the homeless are on the street and teenagers are becoming pregnant with their third child. While the nation is going to war with Iraq, we're arguing whether we should have bishops and archbishops in the Baptist church. Delayed promises can make you distracted. Delayed promises can make you major in minor things and tear up the church over doctrine.

This is a frustrated congregation because they were a people living with unfulfilled promises. Therefore the writer reaches back through Jewish history and begins to exegete Jewish history for a people who have the theological dilemma of delayed promises. The author writes to bolster the hope of the weary, discouraged congregation and to shore up their fledging confidence in this new, risky religion. Jesus had made some promises before he had left, and these people had heard those promises through the disciples and the followers. Now maybe thirty years have passed, and the people are beginning to ask, "How long? When? How will I know?"

What do you do when you know you heard God tell you something, and time passes on? You ask questions when you have been waiting on God. You believed the promises, gave your life for this calling, walked away from everything, and now you wait on the promises of God to be fulfilled. It took David twenty years between the time God anointed him as king and the time he finally got his appointment papers.

Because of the delayed promises, many of these Hebrew Christians have now started to defect and leave the Christian ministry because it is too hard, it is too difficult, and they are not getting the results they were expecting. Some are beginning to reach back to what was safe and conventional and what they had grown up on; some are reaching for what worked and what got a shout and a hallelujah instead of doing the hard work.

The hard work of preaching is standing there even in the absolute silence of people. Preaching even though nobody believes you. Preaching even though they walk out on you. But that's not what we see now. If it's not a mega-situation, we do not believe that it is of God. But the preaching of the gospel is not about success; it is about consistency. It is not about popularity; it is about the loneliest journey of living from the last time you heard from God to the next time you hear from God—and it might be years. What do you do when the bush stops burning? when God grabs your attention with the bush and never speaks to you again? Can you handle the faith with the fulfillment during the not-yet period?

During the not-yet period all you remember is what you think you heard. You're not quite clear anymore about what you heard, but you're so far out here, you've got to keep going. You can't go back because there is really nothing back there for you.

The congregation in this letter to the Hebrews asked, "Why? How long? I thought . . . ?" These are the questions that break the back of the faithful. These are the questions that separate the old saints from the new converts. These are the questions that make mature Christians. And the Bible is full of these questions.

We are lured into this ministry by God's promises, only to discover that God's ways are not our ways. It's a lesson of faith that every generation must confront—wondering if there's something you're doing wrong. Is God still God? Have I been duped? It makes you question your vocation. When I feel especially bewildered about my choices, I find it immeasurably comforting to return to the book of Hebrews, because it stands as a Magna Carta, the founding manifesto of the Christian faith. And it sheds light on the very essence of what it means to be the people of God. The book of Hebrews reminds me of what matters most even when I have questions about my vocation.

Some of the things we encounter in the church make you wonder if your calling is all in vain. You know what it is to live in that delayed season: you look at how you tried to be faithful and tried to do this thing the right way. You tried to follow every scintilla of the law and tried to study the right way. And then you turn and see that—if not the wicked—then certainly the lazy are prospering. Trifling people are prospering, and the inconsistent people are prospering. It makes you want to throw up your hands. You know what it takes to try to have a ministry to the homeless, a tutorial ministry, a battered women's shelter, and a day care. And after you have worked so hard on trying to be faithful about this ministry, trying to be faithful about the theological study, and trying to be faithful about a social justice element in your church, one of your close members sends you an email saying he's leaving the church because he is looking for a deeper word in the Lord. Someone else you've helped is trying to steal your church. You wonder if it's all in vain.

You serve the Lord to the best of your ability, and your teen-age daughter is pregnant. Your son is in jail. The doctors call you in because of a spot on your X-ray. You're behind on your mortgage, and your marriage is a sham. Is it all in vain? You go to divinity school, get training, learn historical criticisms, and figure out what the hermeneutic of suspicion is. You learn about the two creation stories in the book of Genesis, and you wonder how you're going to preach that to the Black folks back at your local church. You go on and you get an MDiv, a DMin, and do all of this training. And here comes a little jackleg in your city who went to an online Bible college—and failed that but still got a degree—and now he's packing out the whole city. You've got to ask yourself, "Is it all worth it?"

And so this little church in the book of Hebrews asked, "Did we get it wrong? Is it all in vain?" They've got factions in this local church. Some are reaching for the past, and then some are trying to be moderates.

Therefore the writer of Hebrews begins to exegete the Old Testament and says, "Let's go through what our ancestors believe." To win back the defecting Christians, the writer drives home four points in the first ten chapters of the book. He explains: (1) the superiority of Jesus Christ to the angels, (2) the superiority of Jesus to the prophets—notably to Moses, who until that time was a prophet par excellence, (3) the superiority of Christ's priesthood to the Leviticus priesthood, and (4) the superiority of the sacrifice of Christ to the animal sacrifices.

The writer says it is not prophets, angels, the priesthood, or human sacrifice. The writer says, "If you're going to reach back for your past, don't go for the angels, the priesthood, the prophets. Go for faith!" That is why the writer says "now" in Heb. 11:1. After the author has eliminated all these things in the ten previous chapters, after the writer has theologically destroyed all these things, the writer says, "Now faith!"

How are you going to live between the last time you heard from God and the next time you hear from God? By faith. Faith is the substance of things hoped for and the evidence of things not seen. You've got to get the faith issue right because this Christian vocation falls and rises on faith. Without faith, it is impossible to please God.

You're going to have to preach to five as though it's five thousand. You're going to have to study even when the registrar says that the check didn't come. You're going to have to pastor through a broken heart. You're going to have to preach that God is a mother to the motherless and a father to the fatherless even though you never met your father and even though your mother walked away. You're going to have to preach it because it's true and not because you've experienced it.

"Now faith is the assurance of things hoped for, the conviction of things not seen" (Heb. 11:1). And then the writer in Heb. 11:4-38 calls out this great hall of faith, as though to say, "In case I'm getting too ethereal on you, let me bring it down home to you."

The author goes on to say that by faith, Abel offered God a better sacrifice than Cain; by faith Enoch forgot to die and was translated from this life to the life to come; by faith Noah, when warned of things to come, began to set out to revere God and to build an ark. By faith Abraham decided to sacrifice his son, Isaac.

Now, all these died in faith, but when history gets written, it's going to say "did not receive what was promised" (v. 39). These ancestors had the faith, but they didn't have the fulfillment. They had the promises of God, but when history gets written, every one of these failed.

Abraham was a man of faith, but he sold his wife as his sister. Sarah got the child that she wanted, but she didn't really believe God down in her soul so she gave her husband an Egyptian maiden. It's an equivocating kind of success. On one level, it's a success, but on another level, it's a failure. It's those blessings that don't bless. It's those blessings that cause more trouble than they solve. I'm talking about how on one level you were a good person, but on another level you were no good.

These all died in faith, but not having received what was promised. When history gets written, Ella Mitchell, you shall die in faith,
not having received what was promised. When my own time is over,
and I have taught at as many seminaries as I care to talk about, and as
they write my name across the pages of history, there will nevertheless be a voice in the background saying, "She died in faith not having
received what was promised." I'm talking about that failure that dogs
your success. I'm talking about those weaknesses that nip away at your
possibilities. I'm talking about that stuff that's half success and half
failure. I'm talking about those successes that feel like failures, but
those failures are redeemed by faith.

These all died in faith not having received what was promised.
Faith is learning how to live between a promise and its fulfillment.
Faith is learning how to live between the now and the not yet. Faith
is learning how to live between the last time you heard from God and
the next time you hear from God. Faith is learning to live between a
vision and its reality. Faith is learning how to live with the silence of
God, learning how to live on nothing but the memory that you think
you heard from God.

And the writer of Hebrews said, "since God had provided something better so that they would not, apart from us, be made perfect."
All of God's "no's" are not the same. There is a "no" that means
never, and there is a "no" that means not yet. The writer says that
God has set up history so that it is not that God condemns Sarah
and Enoch and Abraham to nothing, but that God understands
that there is a not-yet place in history. Somehow or another in the
imagination of God, God has so set this thing up that each generation builds on the generation before it. It did not happen for Sarah
the way she thought it would happen. On one level, time slams the
book down and says "not having received what was promised." But
on another level, there is another book that gets open in the pages
of history that says all of us here today are climbing on the backs of
our ancestors.

Each generation passes the baton to the next generation. If it
were left up to me, I would have been angry and left the ministry a
long time ago. But I have no right to leave the ministry because many
women wanted to be ministers but were not allowed. Every time I
stand, I stand on the shoulders of Jarena Lee and Ella Baker, women
who were faithful to their calling but never saw the fulfillment of
many of the promises.

And one day I'm going to decrease, and the next generation of
little girls are going to increase, and they are going to stand on my

shoulders. When I want to give up, I remember the great cloud of witnesses who surround me and those who will come after me. This race is not about you and me. It's about generations who are coming after us.

Therefore let us run this race with patience, looking to Jesus. And when I get finished, I'm going to pass the baton on to somebody else. And when she gets finished, she's going to pass the baton on to somebody else. And what I don't finish, somebody else is going to finish. And what she doesn't finish, somebody else is going to finish, because we're going to be looking to Jesus, who is the author and the finisher of our faith.

13.

Keep the Pressure On

When You Are the Only One in the Watchtower

Vashti M. McKenzie

One of the culinary memories of my childhood is waiting for the delicacies that would come out of my mama's pressure cooker on the stove. It could be anything from pot roast to pig feet, chili to neck bones. And so I waited with tiptoe anticipation; I waited in the doorway of the kitchen because I had learned from the tales of the elder women in my family that it could be dangerous for children to stand too close to a pressure cooker on the stove.

The pressure cooker was a unique utensil in my mama's arsenal of pots and pans. And it allowed its contents to cook quickly with a high temperature that produced steam in such a volume that it provided pressure upon its contents. You see pressure, beloved, is caused when weight above or around an object exerts a force, and that force can be called pressure. There are gaskets in the pressure cooker—these are rubber seals around the edge of the pot that seal the force inside. And there's a tube that's in the middle of the pot—a steam vent—that allows just the right amount of steam to escape because there is a small weight in a gauge on top of the steam vent that jiggles and does a happy dance to allow the steam to escape.

Now, this pressure cooker is also a dangerous utensil because if the pressure gauge is not set properly, the pot could explode and send the contents all over the kitchen causing bodily harm and certainly a waste of food. But when the gauge is balanced, then the pressure is controlled. And because the pressure is controlled, it forces the food to cook quickly. If the elements are not properly balanced, then the food, the pot, and the kitchen could be destroyed. Thus one wisely stands in the door of the kitchen waiting for the food to be done.

Beloved, so it is with the pressure of our profession as priests and prophets. Some people outside of our profession believe that what we do is a walk in the park. They think that our workweek is filled with nothing but prayer and playing around. They believe that we just study and sit around waiting for the next service to start. They are oblivious to what we do and what we have to go through to get it done. They think that we are just pampered pontificators who are waiting to be served rather than serving.

Beloved, they are oblivious to all of us living in a pressure cooker in the kingdom. Remember the definition—pressure is the weight of something that bears down upon something or around something that exerts a force. And so when God's will bears down on your will, that's pressure. When your way of life fails to intersect with God's Word, that's pressure. When the ministry to the flock conflicts with the ministry to the family, that's pressure. When decisions are made in fear rather than faith, that's pressure. When what you pray for is not what you get, it asserts a pressure. When you carry the cross but want to hold the crown, it's pressure. When the blessings of the call meet the burden of preparation for the call, that's pressure. When the expectations of others combine with your own personal expectations and what you believe God expects of you, that's pressure.

Moses was under pressure because of his murmuring mega-congregation who wanted to be free without the inconvenience of being free. He had to delegate work to somebody else. Paul was under pressure just trying to reach Jerusalem. Titus, a brand-new pastor, was under pressure trying to serve a hard and unruly people. Elijah was under pressure and ran from Ahab and Jezebel. King Herod had to yield to pressure and washed his hands on the eve of the crucifixion. Esther, our sister girlfriend, was under pressure between who she was and who she'd become and Haman's genocidal scheme. Potipher's wife put Joseph under pressure. In case you don't know now, there is pressure in our profession.

There is the pressure of perfection. We must live perfect lives, have perfect families, live in perfect houses, have perfect wardrobes, with perfect appointments and perfect lifestyles. We must be God's Exhibit A, God's role model—preacher, pastor, and servant.

If it's not the pressure of perfection, it is the pressure of originality. Everyone who sits under your preaching and teaching expects it to be brand-new, even though we're working from the same reference book, the same material. Yet you must be an original every time, no matter how many commentaries you read. There is also the pressure of being relevant—taking what was written to ancient people in an agricultural age and retooling it for the twenty-first century, coding it in a delivery system so that it is received without sacrificing truth.

What pressure? We have the pressure of performance because we are in a let-me-entertain-you age where church can't happen without staging and video screens and sound bites. Let's push the altar aside, remove the cross. It is let-me-entertain-you time. You can't stand behind the pulpit anymore; you've got to come out. You've got to jump a bit. You've got to dance a bit. You've got to prance a bit. It's the pressure of performance.

Then there is the privacy issue—you have none. And the pressure of our humanity—we are under pressure of the same social conditions, the same temptations. We are vulnerable even as the ones we preach to are vulnerable, but we must live under a different set of standards. We've got pressure.

We need someone to help us with this issue of pressure. And so the lot falls to John the Baptist, who seems now to be one who has handled the pressure of the perfection before the pressure handled him. We see in Mark 1:4-8 how John also kept the pressure on in his community.

What kind of pressure did John have? Well, he was perhaps under pressure to be just like everybody else, although he couldn't be. Can you imagine this young man? He couldn't play ball like all the rest of the young men, could not hang out at the mall, couldn't sneak cigarettes outside of school buildings, couldn't dance the night away at the club, for he was an ordained Nazarite. And can you imagine him now being under pressure?—the secular nature of his environment pressing in upon his sacred call.

John was pressured to produce with few resources. Look at the text. It says that he was assigned to the wilderness AME, Baptist, Pentecostal, Apostolic, Presbyterian, and Church of God in Christ. He was assigned to the west side of the Dead Sea in a wild wilderness area where very few people lived. And so he was assigned to do the work of the Lord where there were very few people.

And then there was the pressure of potential. John had a special birth announced and foretold by an angel to a womb believed barren. The potential was great. There was the expectation that this son—the only son in this priestly family—was going to be somebody. He had pressure to do something, to make his mark and impact upon religious life and to affect the community. For it had been a long time since there was an authentic word from the Lord. And yet Mark says there was "a voice crying in the wilderness."

The Gospel of Mark begins abruptly with a proclamation of the divinity of Jesus; he proclaims Jesus as "the Son of God." Then Mark further introduces Christ by spending a moment on the forerunner of the Christ—that is John the Baptist, the prophet under pressure.

This prophet kept pressure on his community. He ate honey and locust; he did not do power lunches with salad, fried chicken, greens, and sweet potatoes. This prophet was a little weirder than the others. You may call him a geek. This prophet's resume was not encouraging. Some scholars say that John had a "no-nonsense" approach to his call. In other words, he needed to work on his people skills. He was not affected by title or heritage. But in spite of all the negatives that could be launched on John's side, Mark 1:5 says that all of Jerusalem came out to hear John; he heard their confession, and they repented and were baptized. All of the people came out from Jerusalem, which makes a good point. People will go where their needs are met. And so although John didn't look like the rest of the boys and he had a church on the other side of town and he did not participate in the ministerial alliance and he was subject to all of the pressures of the profession, John was still able to apply the pressure on those who were around him.

How did John do it? John was focused. His diet, his demands, his actions were all centered upon his purpose and mission. He was not sidetracked. He was not distracted. He preached an unbroken record: "Repent and be baptized. . . . The Messiah is coming."

I had a seminary professor who said we preach one sermon all of our lives. It matters not the text, it matters not the exegesis, but we're all simply preaching the same sermon again and again and again. John was able to apply pressure in his community because everything he did was focused to accomplish his mission and goal. He didn't water it down. It was a tough call. It was a tough message. John remained strong, and the testimony is that the people followed and came to the west side of the Dead Sea.

But more than that, John was more concerned about being heard than he was about anything else. We too will be heard when we get focused. Live right. Speak the truth in love. Act like a neighbor. Do your work; get your job done; pay your bills; be faithful to the spouse you have; take care of your responsibilities. If you mess up, then clean up. If you make a mistake, then say you are sorry. Do your part. Carry your weight. Shoulder your load. Speak words that are of God. And as Paul wrote to the church of Thessalonica, "take care of your own business." Do your own work, and the people will come great distances to hear.

How was John able to survive the pressures of the profession and yet maintain pressure on the community? He didn't become a part of the crowd to get a crowd; he didn't lower his standards to change the crowd. He wasn't trying to fit in to get in; he didn't become a part of the world, but he wanted to have an impact on it. He wasn't trying to be a chameleon changing the color with each changing whim and each changing fad. But John maintained his standards of living and loving an awesome God.

People may not love you because you maintain high standards; you may not win a lot of friends because you stand on the high standards of God. They may not love you, but they will respect you for where you stand. John is our example. He survived the pressure of his profession and applied pressure in his community because he wasn't afraid to stand alone. There was one voice crying in the wilderness. There was no other support. You may be the only watchman in the tower. You may be the only one on the wall. You may be the only voice crying in the wilderness, but you've got to keep your courage up. Be brave and bold and speak up for God. Otherwise the pressure of politics will overwhelm you. You'll spend more time asking yourself: "What should I say? Should I say it now? Who do I need to be friends with? Who do I need to stand with? They're in trouble. I've got to get away from them. They're rising up. I've got to stay with them. When do I announce who or which presidential candidate I'm supporting? Do I wade in now or do I wade in later?" No, John didn't go through all of those things. But he was willing to stand alone. For if you stand alone, God will never leave you nor forsake you.

Last, remember that John—who navigated the pressures of the profession and kept the pressure on his community—practiced what he preached and matched what he said with what he did. If John had preached repentance and lived immorally, if John had called for holiness and he had a dishonest reputation, if his word had not matched his life, everybody would have stayed home, and no one would have come to the west side of the Dead Sea. The people are more interested sometimes in what we do than what we say. They are watching us every day—examining us closely in our personal life and in our congregational life. They want to know how we are applying scripture to our personal life.

And the text said when he did all of that, the people came flocking out of Jerusalem. It's a testimony for us. Pressure can wear you out. Pressure can make your heart feeble. Pressure can make you restless in your spirit. Pressure can drain your resources. Pressure can bankrupt you spiritually. Pressure can break the best of us and depress the rest of us. But John understood the right balance of pressure. He was focused on what God had called him to do. He wasn't focused on anybody else's ministry except for what God had called him to do. He didn't become a part of the crowd to get a crowd or to change a crowd. He wasn't afraid to stand alone. He understood his relationship with Christ. He wasn't the Christ but the forerunner. He was to handle water, and Jesus was to handle fire, and he practiced what he preached.

And so now as we go out into the wilderness to do the work that God has for us to do, we cannot fall under pressure of our profession, but like John, we must keep up the pressure in our community. We must keep the pressure on a nation that can find billions of dollars to rebuild Afghanistan and Iraq but cannot find enough money to rebuild our educational institutions. We have got to keep the pressure on when millions are trying to live without health care and the prescriptions cost more than Social Security. We have got to keep the pressure on when we live in a country where a war hero like Shoshana Johnson, a Black prisoner of war, has to fight for 30 percent disability, when they give another soldier, Jessica Lynch, a white woman, 80 percent disability.[1] We have to keep the pressure on when we live in a place where a white detective can conduct an undercover antidrug operation in Texas, and the only folk who are arrested are Black, married to Black people, dating Black people, or are high school athletic stars.[2] We have got to remain focused, and what we preach, we've got to live.

The pressure of our profession—we must make sure that it doesn't handle us but that we handle it. And at the same time, we must keep the pressure on our communities.

14.

Communion

An Act of Revolution
and a Call to Solidarity

James A. Forbes Jr.

Ever since the terrorists attacked the World Trade Center in New York on September 11, 2001, people in the United States have never been the same. After the attacks we as a people, as a nation, entered into a season of vulnerability, panic, pain, and perplexity. As a result perhaps the largest prayer meeting ever took place in this nation. Because in the light of September 11, heaven saw that the switchboard was jammed with prayers coming in, in a concert for the nation when it sang, "God Bless America." That was the prayer, and heaven received it. God answered: "I am going to come down and bless America." I know God answered because one Sunday morning when they were trying to clear the wreckage from Ground Zero (the site of the tragedy that left thousands dead), something unusual happened that I assume was God's answer to the prayer. Out of the rubble—after they had determined that no life could be left there anymore—a white pigeon flew up. People could not explain where the living pigeon came from. How did it happen? There was no life left down there, and yet the pigeon came up.

And of course, given my background, I was very much sure that God was answering the question, "How can America be blessed?" America can only be blessed if there is a mighty spiritual revitalization. Now some of the biblical scholars may ask me, "Well, what about the pigeon? It does not represent spiritual revitalization." Well, my response to them would be, "In a crisis like that, if you can't get a dove, a pigeon will have to do."

The pigeon came forth, and I was convinced that this was God's way of saying, "America, apart from a mighty spiritual revitalization of values, you will not be blessed."

God continues to say, "But don't worry. I think I've got some folks who will be able to help you understand what this means. I've got a church that I have raised up, a church that I have nourished with the idea that military might will not do it, a church that has studied deeply into Zechariah, and they know 'it's not by might, nor by power but by my spirit saith the Lord.'" And so the Lord was going to answer the prayer of America.

But there was a problem. The problem was that the church had lost its prophetic power. The church was silent most of the time. The church had acquired an immunity deficiency. The church in America had AIDS—a spiritual AIDS. I'm not going to talk about T cells, which are associated with the physical disease known as AIDS. I'm going to talk about the C-count; the church's C-count was low. The C-count that I'm speaking of is courage. You can't be a church if your C-count is low. You can't be the church with a low C-count. You might as well call yourself something else.

Therefore, we are gathered at the Samuel DeWitt Proctor Conference to make sure we raise the C-count in the church. When we leave this conference, we can say that we've been to the Proctor Conference for Prophetic Encouragement.

Let's look at two biblical models of prophetic courage. The first model is Esther. Mordecai said to Esther, "Honey, you're not safe just because you're in the king's palace. If you don't find some courage from somewhere, you might discover that you and your people will go down the drain."

So I see Esther as one who stands before us at this time to help us understand what the Proctor Conference for Prophetic Encouragement is all about. She had been nourished. She was a person who had lost both of her parents. She then went to live with Uncle Mordecai. And she was raised by Uncle Mordecai, and I guess there was an Aunt Mordecai—you know in the Bible we often leave the other half out. When trouble came to that little girl with her parents gone, maybe they said, "Pretty little Esther, go out and play; Auntie and I are going to fast and pray." Esther was nourished.

Then we hear her asking, "Uncle Mordecai, why? Why do we have to move again? They're kicking us out, but God will take us in." That little child was learning so much, and then when she was finally in the location, she figured out she had a vocation. Here is a woman who has to engage in possible civil disobedience at the cost of her life.

Well, what happened is that she said, "If I perish, I perish." Oh, Esther, how can you get those words in our mouths today? If we follow the agenda that's been set forth here at this conference, somebody is going to perish before it's all over. But we should follow Esther's lead: "If I perish, I perish."

Furthermore, there's another example. His name is Jesus. I see Jesus going down to be baptized by John and then something happens to help his courage along. In fact Jesus was born with courage. The stuff was already in him. But when he was on Mary and Joseph's lap, the family and the family of faith gave him courage as a little boy. Even at the age of twelve, he didn't have to hang around. He could venture out and say, "Must I not be about my father's business?"

And it turns out that that day when he went to be baptized by John, he really received the ultimate endorsement. When he came up out of the water, heaven said: "This is my beloved Son with whom I'm well pleased." That gave him courage to stand up, and he was going to need it. He needed it when he went back home to stand up before those people and say, "The spirit of the Lord is upon me." It took courage. It took courage to say it in the first place. In fact he changed a little bit of what it was saying. He left out the vengeance part and went on down the way. And before it was all over, they drove him to the edge of the town to try to kill the brother.

Some of us at this conference are going to be led to the edge of the hill. Therefore it is important for me to say to you that you've been to the Conference for Prophetic Encouragement.

It is likely that this conference will be the place that history records a second Civil Rights revolution in America.

So let me tell you what we need to do as we remember Christ through communion. Remember, it was at the table when Jesus got ready to face the situation that would bring a revolution in creation itself. When we take communion, it shouldn't be ordinary. Don't you dare take that cup unless you understand that this cup is encouragement. It is not feel-good encouragement but prophetic encouragement. It gives you the courage to stand with Esther and say, "If I perish, I perish."

Don't you dare touch this communion cup unless you are planning to go home and do something that makes it possible for this nation to know that God heard the prayer we cried out after September 11. I tell you I have no choice myself to carry the Word, because of two things.

First, a table is where the encouragement came from. Ask Dr. King about the table. Stand up, Martin! Stand up for righteousness and justice. Now the problem was—that was then. He got that at his kitchen table. But now the Lord's got us out here at a family communion service. Your table is not enough for this. Solidarity is necessary. Don't you dare touch it unless you're going to do something about it.

Second, I have got to do something because of my ancestor, C. C. Forbes. You don't know him. I didn't know about him until recently. But you can know that he was down at a slave plantation on Route 58 between Snow Hill and Stantonburg. C. C. Forbes was a preacher to slaves. He preached to the slaves down in the bush harbor. When the boss came down, the slave master shot him in the leg and said, "You can't preach here anymore." The slave master said to him, "Don't you come down here no more. I shot you in the leg as a warning that if you preach anymore, I'm going to kill you." C. C. Forbes stood up on that shot leg and said, "Well, you just as well go 'head and shoot me now because I'll be back. I'm going to preach here until I die. Go ahead and kill me anyhow!" That's what my ancestor said. And the slave master was so dumbfounded by this courage that he said, "Alright, go ahead. Y'all can have this little plot of land."

Now if you go down to Route 58 by Stantonburg, you'll see that Baptist church C. C. Forbes built and preached in. What does that mean? It means that if you have courage, some of us may get shot. If you have courage, we may be investigated. But don't worry; God's going to make a way. That's why I wish you all would pray for me because it's in my blood. It's on the table, and I know I've got to go. Encourage my soul, and let me journey on. Though the night be dark, it won't be very long. Thanks be to God; the storm is passing over.

15.

A Prophetic Witness in an Anti-Prophetic Age

Otis Moss Jr.

JESUS CHRIST SHOWS US THE ULTIMATE EXAMPLE of how we are to deliver a prophetic word and be prophetic witnesses in an anti-prophetic age. It is amazing that Jesus—after being protected in Africa among people who looked like him—came back to Nazareth and decided to go to a normal gathering, an ordinary gathering, and brought to it an extraordinary, unexpected prophetic word (Luke 4:18). The people in the synagogue simply gave him a document. The King James Version says they gave him a book, but we know that is not true. They gave him a scroll out of the prophetic tradition, what we now called the sixty-first chapter of Isaiah. The synagogue leaders told Jesus to read the text, and he started reading it, and then he preached a sermon shorter than the text. He said, "This day is this scripture fulfilled in your hearing." Then he sat down, according to the record. What a sermon! Have you ever preached a sermon shorter than your text? Then they engaged in a brief dialogue. Before the dialogue was over, he almost got killed just talking about the sermon.

How often have our lives been threatened for having dialogue about the sermon we just delivered? We are not in particular danger because we have too often adjusted to this anti-prophetic age; there is no danger in the sermons we preach, no challenge, and no threat to anybody. But Jesus almost got killed on perhaps his first public sermon. We should remember that the community, the world, does not like prophets, and neither does the church. Prophets disturb us. They shake us out of our dogmatic slumber. So we prefer comfort to commitment. The world does not like prophets. They override our creeds and our half-truths. They expose our injustices and our contradictions and put to shame our mediocrity. The world does not like prophets, and the church often refuses to celebrate them.

We all have Dr. King's photograph on our walls. But I was there when his own denomination excommunicated him and—in the words of Gardner Taylor—"denied him a home address." In his own denomination King was vice president of the National Baptist Sunday School and BTU Congress, which is now the Christian Education Congress. But by the tyrannical acts of a few people, King was removed without a vote from that position and made unwelcome. After this happened, I stood with tears in my eyes, and I heard not a member of the Ku Klux Klan, but a brother who looks like us say, "He's got everything; he's on the cover page of *Time* magazine. Every time I open the newspaper, he's in it. Every time I turn on the television, he's on it. Give us something."

We don't like prophets. Dr. King gave his final message to the Progressive National Baptist Convention against the war in Vietnam. In less than a year, he would be assassinated. I was the regional representative of the Southern Christian Leadership Conference, and Dr. Abernathy called me and said, "Otis, here's what we want you to do. Go out and get five thousand leaflets printed and put on it the time that Dr. King is going to speak to the convention and give the subject: The War in Vietnam and the Christian Conscience." He told me to put this on the leaflet and distribute it throughout the convention and the Cincinnati community. Before I could get to the printer, I got a telephone call that I did not return because the spirit told me that it was a call that I wanted to get later. So I had all of the leaflets printed up and got some young people from our congregation to help distribute them, and then I took the call. The call came from a high official in our convention—I'm talking about the Progressive National Convention. The official called me and said, "You have a relationship with Dr. King. Please tell him not to speak on Vietnam. Some of the brethren won't like it." Well, by that time I had already sent out the leaflets. I said, "Well, I'll tell you, I can't talk to him because I don't know where he is. He's on his way here, and the leaflets are already out. Why don't we just pray?"

And on that occasion Dr. King spoke. After he spoke, the Progressive National Baptist Convention unanimously endorsed or adopted a resolution against the war in Vietnam. We had written the resolution earlier in Dr. King's hotel room. This was the last time he spoke to the Progressive National Baptist Convention, but there was a handful of ministers who left before he spoke. He was not wanted in Atlanta.

I was in Atlanta when the announcement went out that Martin Luther King Jr. was moving from Montgomery, Alabama, to Atlanta, Georgia, where he was born. Ernest Vandiver, the governor of Georgia at that time, called a press conference in the state capitol and said, "Martin Luther King Jr. is not welcome in Georgia." And then a Black reporter from *Atlanta Daily World*, a Black newspaper, went throughout the community interviewing—not white folk—but Black folk. The reporter asked, "What do you think about Dr. King's coming to Atlanta?" Leader number one said "no comment." Leader number two: "I don't want to get into that controversy." Leader number three: "We've already got enough leaders in Atlanta." Dr. King was not wanted in his own hometown. So King was bombed in Montgomery; jailed in Birmingham, Albany, and St. Augustine; stoned in Chicago; invited out of town in Cleveland; and unwanted in Atlanta.

But the spirit of the Lord was upon him. And if I could rephrase it, I would say, he was wounded for his nation's transgressions, bruised for America's iniquities, and the burdens of Black people and white people and all people were upon his shoulders. And because he was a prophet, we can all stand a little taller and walk the earth with a little more dignity. He gave teachers more to teach and preachers more to preach. He made newspapers worth reading and television worth watching. Why? Because the spirit of the Lord was upon him. God told him to proclaim the good news.

If we look closely at this text, we see how holistic Jesus' ministry was. He said, "the spirit of the Lord is upon me. . . . God has anointed me [that has to be theological] to proclaim good news to the poor [I believe that's economics]." He goes on to say that God told him to get "release to the captives," which must be political. "To recover the sight of the blind" is educational and sociological. "To let the oppressed go free" is liberation theology. And then, to proclaim the year of jubilee, "to proclaim the year of the Lord's favor" is theological.

So at the top of Jesus' text is theology, and in between it is economics, politics, and sociology. Then at the bottom it's theology. Therefore if you are preaching a gospel that has nothing about politics, nothing about economics, nothing about sociology, you are preaching an empty gospel with a cap and shoes but no body to it. It might be a popular gospel, but it's not powerful. It might be expedient, but it's not saving. It might be safe, but it's not saving. We need prophets in this age in which prophets are not liked. We need prophets of peace—and

I didn't say peaceful prophets. Prophets of peace understand why we could have taken medicine to Iraq and not bombs.

Unfortunately, the church has allowed generals of the army to become more prophetic than we are. Field Marshal Haag said, "It's the business of the church to make my business impossible." I'm not quoting Amos and Hosea and Micah; I'm quoting generals of the army. General H. H. Arnold said, "We won the last war [talking about World War II], and it is the last war we will ever win. For in a nuclear age, victory is no longer possible. War itself is defeat." General Omar Bradley, who admitted that he was not even a registered voter, said, "We have too many men of science and too few men of God. We know more about killing than we know about living. We know more about making war than we know about making peace. We live in an age of nuclear giants and ethical infants." And General Douglas MacArthur, who was perhaps at the bottom of his being a racist, said, "War should be outlawed." General Sherman is reported to have said—we're not sure that he said it—but allegedly said: "War is hell." And it is.

And the prophet said, "Nation shall not lift up sword against nation. Neither shall they learn war anymore." We need prophets of peace. I know where the weapons of mass destruction are, and they are not the ones we went looking for in Iraq. I know where they are, and you know where they are! According to statistics, AIDS is a weapon of mass destruction. Miseducation and no education are weapons of mass destruction. Forty-four million people without health care is a weapon of mass destruction. Children with good minds and no money to go to school are weapons of mass destruction. People who have done no wrong living outdoors and under bridges this morning are weapons of mass destruction. And the prophet said, "Come unto me all ye that labor and are heavy laden and I will give you rest."

Wyatt Walker told me that he named his twenty-fifth book *My Stroke of Grace*. I said, "Wyatt, why did you give it that title?" He said, "Well, there was a battle going on in my body. I was about to have a heart attack and didn't know it. And I was about to have a stroke at the same time. There was a physiological, biological struggle going on in my body, and the stroke won out over the heart attack. If I'd had both, I wouldn't be here. And since I had the stroke, I was able to write about my stroke of grace."

Wyatt's story reminds me of E. Stanley Jones, who had a stroke in his eighties and got up and wrote a book entitled *The Divine Yes*. If you are a prophet, you will see something and seek something and say something and do something that is strange and abnormal to the general public. The prophet will hear something that others are not hearing.

Isaiah said that in the year that King Uzziah died, "I saw." I don't know how many people were in the temple on that occasion, but Isaiah said, "I saw." And I'm not sure that everybody else saw what Isaiah saw, even though they were in the same temple. Maybe they were in the same pew, but they didn't see what he saw. Isaiah saw something.

I come from the country, and I have country illustrations. There was a young woman who was working in a restaurant, and one day when she went to work they were expecting a large turnout because it was a day before a holiday. They cooked an extraordinary supply of chicken, but the expected company and customer base didn't come. So toward the end of the day when she had already worked overtime, the proprietor of the restaurant told her to take some of the chicken home. But by this time she had missed her last bus and had to walk home in the dark. As she walked home with this big bag of chicken in the dark, somebody moved out of a dark alley and put a choke hold around her neck and dragged her down the alley. And she said a strange thing: "While the attacker was dragging me, I heard a voice that said to take out a piece of chicken and eat it." Imagine being dragged down an alley by an attacker, and a voice says take out a piece of chicken and eat it. And, strangely enough, the woman obeyed the voice. While she was taking out the chicken, there were two hungry alley dogs down the alley fighting in a garbage can. But when she pulled the chicken out of the bag, the aroma got caught up on the wings of angels and moved down the alley and captured the attentions and the appetites of the hungry dogs. They came charging down the alley, growling and ready to fight; her attacker turned her loose and ran away. And she gave a little chicken to the dogs. For the rest of her journey as she walked home, she would take a little piece of the chicken out of the bag and give it to these alley dogs.

You know the Twenty-Third Psalm, "Yea, though I walk through the valley," but drop the "v" and say, "Yea, though I walk through the alley of the shadow of death, I will fear no evil," because God can take alley dogs and make them guardian angels. God's prophets, go out and proclaim the year of jubilee!

IV

Witnesses for All Generations

16.

Born to Be a Witness

Samuel "Billy" Kyles

DREAMERS ARE THE ONES who make the world go around. They are not afraid to step outside of the box. They go after "it." Langston Hughes says: "Hold fast to dreams / For if dreams die / Life is a broken-winged bird / That cannot fly. // Hold fast to dreams."[1]

Every five years I try to do something dramatic and spectacular for our wedding anniversary. The last five years I asked my darling, "How would you like to go to the Polynesian Islands? Fiji, Bora Bora, Tahiti?" She says, "Oh yes, yes, yes, I'd like to go."

I got two business-class tickets to Tahiti. At the airport, they bumped us up to first class. I didn't ask any questions; I just said, "Thank you very much." We got on this airplane—a 747—and there's only about sixteen seats in first class. First class was awesome. I looked at this huge airplane, and as the jet pulls back and you go to the runway, this thing with all of its weight, with all of its passengers, with the food, the fuel, and the luggage, with all of that—this thing goes down the runway and in less than two minutes this hotel on wheels takes off into the wild blue yonder. I do not see a sign that says Tahiti straight ahead. All I see is blue sky and clouds. They wake you up in the morning eight and a half hours later, and we land in Tahiti—not in Australia, not in Fiji, not in Hawaii. We land in Tahiti.

How did they do that? Well, there's a person on the plane whose only responsibility is to go from point A to point B. This person is called a flight engineer. And the flight engineer deals with a flight plan. Even with the flight plan, the flight engineer might have to make adjustments. He might get word that bad weather is ahead. He'll either go over it or go around it or go under it, but he does not go back. I am suggesting that we need a flight plan for our lives; otherwise, we might just land anywhere.

I mentioned the airplane story because that was somebody's dream. We all have dreams. Some of us are living our dreams; some of us have lost our dream. Let me encourage you to recapture that dream. What do you think happened when the inventors of the airplane, the Wright brothers, went and told somebody, "Guess what? We're going to invent an airplane." Supposed they had listened to what others said and given up?

Because they held fast to their dream, one day in a little place called Kitty Hawk, North Carolina, that dream became a reality. Can you imagine the world without air travel? Right now there is a space station—not a satellite—a space station orbiting the earth with human beings living on it because of their dream—they would not give up. A man has placed his footprints on the moon.

We know about Martin Luther King's dream. But we know it in the light of today. When Martin was dreaming that dream, it was as foreign to people as the airplane dream. Imagine his audacity; he had a dream that one day his four children would be judged by the content of their character rather than the color of their skin. And can't you hear the dream buster saying, "No, they won't"?

When he was dreaming that dream, neither King nor his children could go into downtown Atlanta, sit on a stool, and eat a hot dog. Yet he kept on dreaming. He couldn't stay in hotels, couldn't go in restaurants, couldn't go but to designated Negro schools, and yet he had the audacity to keep on dreaming that the sons and daughters of slaves and slave owners would sit down at the table of brotherhood. The dream buster said, "No, they won't." But now we do. Hold fast to your dream.

Did slaves have dreams? Yes, they had dreams! You can hear it in the songs. "Yes, there is trouble now, but I'm so glad trouble ain't g'on last always." They had dreams.

While I was in Philadelphia a few years ago, a young woman came up to me and said, "Reverend Kyles, I just want to say thank you for all that you've done and all of us you've helped. I'm a judge here in Philadelphia. I am a judge in my third term, and I'm from Memphis. You don't know me, but I want to say thanks to you and all those who made my dreams come true. I'm a judge, and my daddy was a garbageman."

Our foreparents had dreams. It is said that only five of twenty survived the Middle Passage—that journey from Africa to America. If that's true, then we are descendants of the five, and we owe it to our ancestors to dream big dreams. You'd better believe I do! Those five out of twenty were brought here against their will, and they couldn't speak this language. Can you imagine that? They had no rights, just like cattle in the field. They didn't have bilingual classes to teach our foreparents this language. They didn't speak this language, but they had such a will to live that they learned the language phonetically. They didn't know they were learning it phonetically. They just learned it.

I tell young people as I go around the country, "Don't you be upset when you hear grandmamma say, 'Now you gimme dis h'er' or 'U'm g'on git you.'" They didn't have time to say, "I'm going to get you." They had nothing, but they had a will to live. They are a prime example of the Lord making a way out of no way. Our ancestors took the scraps and the throw-aways, the inner parts of the hog and the pig's feet and all of that, and lifted it to a culinary art. They have chitterlings in Paris now. They took day-old and week-old bread and doctored it up and made bread pudding. I know some places sell bread pudding for seven dollars a slice—our ancestors' same recipe. They didn't have high, medium, or low dials on the stove; they just put it in the oven, and the bread and the biscuits came out just right.

Can you imagine it being illegal to know how to read? The only trouble white people got in regarding black slaves was teaching them how to read, and many did get into trouble teaching slaves how to read.

In less than 140 years, we have gone from it being illegal for us to know how to read to our being everywhere. As I speak to you now, the secretary of state of the most powerful country in the world is African American. I've got to check out his party, but he's still secretary of state. Condoleeza Rice is national security adviser—in less than 150 years from it being illegal for us to know how to read. We now have a holiday in honor of an African American—less than 150 years since it's been legal to read. There have only been four holidays named after individuals—George Washington, Abraham Lincoln, Christopher Columbus, and Martin Luther King Jr. And no matter what your beliefs might be, you've got to deal with the holiday because you will not have mail delivered, the post office is closed, the bank is closed, the stock market is closed, the schools are closed. You've got to deal with it!

Hold fast to your dreams for if dreams die, we're like broken winged birds that cannot fly. Even now, we were enslaved longer than we've been out of slavery. So as horrible as the slavery story is, that is not all of it. Turn over on the other side. The other side is that it took a strong, determined people to survive that madness. And everything that was put before us, we have survived. What a mighty God!

Garbage workers have dreams? Oh, come on. Garbage workers? They don't have any dreams; they just take away the stuff that we throw away. There's a powerful sign from the Sanitation Workers' strike; you'll see it if you go to the Civil Rights Museum in Memphis. It doesn't say peace; it doesn't say freedom; it doesn't say justice. All it says is: "I AM A MAN." Garbage workers were treated less than men. They worked all day, all the week long, and could still qualify for welfare. They had no place to wash after handling garbage all day. For their lunch, they'd sit on the sidewalk and eat bologna sandwiches or Vienna sausages. They had no toilet privileges unless some kind person along the route would let them use theirs. But who wanted the garbagemen in their bathrooms? And so they went on strike. The community had to run to catch up with them. The leadership had to run to catch up with them. We got rallies going, and finally we got to the rally stage where we wanted to get Martin Luther King to come in. His staff said, "We don't have time. We're behind on the Poor People's Campaign." And Martin overruled them and said, "Oh, no, we're going to Memphis. We're going to help the garbage workers realize their dreams."

So he came and made a great speech and came back to lead a march, and that march broke up in violence and he was so hurt. That's why all the staff had come into Memphis and said that we're going to have a peaceful march in Memphis. So he came back into Memphis on April 3—the last trip into Memphis—in preparation for the march.

The mountaintop speech that you've heard about almost didn't take place. There were tornado warnings that night. It was raining and thundering and lightning, and he thought that there would not be many people at the church. So King sent several of us—me, Jesse Jackson, and Ralph Abernathy—to the church. He said, "You guys go over and have the meeting, and I'm going to stay here and work on the Poor People's Campaign." When we got there, the church was nearly full. Jesse walked in, Ralph walked in, I walked in, and others walked in, and the people started clapping. Ralph said, "These people ain't clapping for us; they think Martin's coming in behind us." So he went to the phone and called Martin and said, "Man, you should get over here. These people have come in the weather to hear you."

We almost missed the mountaintop speech, but Martin came on over. He didn't take a topic that night. He just started talking—speaking from his heart. Interestingly enough, Ralph introduced him for twenty minutes. He had no way of knowing that would be the last introduction of his life. But throughout the twenty-minute introduction, nobody said a word, not one word. And Martin teased when he got up, "I thought Dr. Abernathy was going to make a speech." He just started speaking from his heart. I never heard him talk about death as much as he did that night. His plane from Atlanta had been late because it was under guard all night, and they had more death threats, so they had to search the luggage again. He came into Memphis, and there were death threats against his life.

He talked about the time when he was in New York autographing books and a demented Black woman came up to him and said, "Are you Martin Luther King Jr.?" When he said yes, she plunged a letter opener right into his chest. During the speech, he shared the most telling note from a young girl, who wrote, "Dear Dr. King, I read about your misfortune, and I'm so sorry. The *New York Times* said the blade of the letter opener was so close to your aorta that if you had sneezed, you would have drowned in your own blood. I'm so glad that you didn't sneeze."

He picked up on this little girl's line, and he did an entire litany. "And I'm glad I didn't sneeze. If I had sneezed, I would have missed the Selma to Montgomery march. If I had sneezed, I would have missed the Voting Rights Act. If I had sneezed, I would have missed the young people sitting in all over the South for their rights. If I had sneezed, I would have missed a chance to tell America and the world about a dream that I had."

We were on our feet. We were crying, but we didn't know what was making us cry. He said, "I may not get there with you, but you'll get to the Promise Land. Because God has allowed me to go up on the mountain, and I have looked over and I have seen the Promise Land. I may not get there with you, but you'll get there."

And so, my friends, I'm certain he knew he wouldn't get there, but he wouldn't tell us that. Can you imagine what we would have felt had he said straight out to us, "I won't get there"? So he softened it and said, "I may not get there," knowing full well that he wouldn't get there.

He closed, "Tonight, I'm not fearing any man. My eyes have seen the coming of the glory of the Lord. . . ." He didn't finish the quote—although he always finished his quotes—and we had to help him to his seat.

Dinner was to be served at my home the next day; King was in a jovial mood. It is as though he had preached himself through the fear of death. Earlier in the day, he and Andrew Young had a pillow fight.

I told him dinner was at five o'clock because we had a rally that night. He called the house, and they told him the correct time was six. So when I went to get him at five, he said, "Oh no, dinner is at six, and I am in no hurry." That gave me the awesome privilege to spend with him the last hour of his life on earth. Three preachers were gathered in a room—Abernathy, King, and Kyles. Our discussions were very lighthearted.

Ralph needed an evangelist for the week. Martin said, "Why don't you get Kyles?" I said, "I'll be in Columbus, Georgia, preaching for Fred Lofton." Martin looked me dead in the eye and said, "Anybody with good sense would rather spend a week preaching in the city of Atlanta than Columbus, Georgia." I said, "Does that mean that I don't have good sense?" He said: "That's not what I said. Listen to what I said." And he repeated it. Lighthearted.

I had recently purchased a new house, and he said, "Did you buy a new house?" I said, "Yes, I'm buying it." He said: "Well, don't be like that preacher in Atlanta—and I'm not going to call his name; he invited Coretta and me to dinner. We went to his house, and he didn't have any furniture, and we had to eat on a card table. The Kool-Aid was hot, and the ham was cold. Now, if I go to your house and you ain't got no furniture or no food, I'm going to broadcast it all over the nation." Lighthearted.

About a quarter of six we walked on the balcony. Jesse had brought a van in from Chicago. Martin said, "Jesse, don't take that whole van down to Kyles's house—and plus you're not dressed for dinner." Even then Jesse had a sharp mouth; he replied, "I don't need a shirt and tie; I've got an appetite."

And so they started walking toward the balcony. He was leaning over the balcony—the railing of the balcony; I turned and walked away. When I got about four or five steps, the shots rang out. People were ducking in the courtyard. They didn't know if he would continue to shoot. I looked back and saw Martin. That bullet had knocked him from the railing back onto the balcony. He was speaking to Jesse when the bullet hit him. I ran to his side. There was a tremendous hole in the side of his face. There was a bigger wound under his shirt that we could not see. But the bullet was a dum-dum. It didn't go in straight; it mushroomed and tore all of his chest out. I ran in the room and picked up the phone to call an ambulance. The phone was operator assisted, and the operator had left the switchboard when she heard the shot. When she realized that Martin had been shot, she had a heart attack and fell in the courtyard. She died about four days later. She was the motel owner's wife.

I ran back outside. The police were coming by this time. I hollered to them: "Call an ambulance on your police radio. Dr. King has been shot." They said, "Where did the shots come from?" There is a famous picture of people pointing in the direction of the shot. They came and secured the balcony. They called the ambulance. We finally got somebody on the switchboard. I suggested to Jesse we call Mrs. King and I would call my home, and we waited and we waited. Finally, the word came that Martin Luther King Jr. had been officially pronounced dead after being shot on the balcony of the Lorraine Motel.

I cannot tell you my feelings even now—standing next to him one moment and seeing him in that shape another moment. I have no words to express it. I waited. I wondered, "Why was I there?" We could have been in so many other places. We were young pastors and young friends. But why was I there at that moment in time—frozen in time? And God revealed it to me over the years. It was like the unfolding of a flower. I don't know how long it took, but it came to me as a revelation. If you give the flower time to unfold on its own, you'll have a beautiful flower. If you try to rush it, you tear the petals off and you destroy the flower. So, I waited.

When the revelation came to me, it was like laying a heavy burden down. I was there to be a witness. Here I am—thirty-five years later—witnessing to young people who were not even born at the time and their parents were perhaps children. And my witness has to be true. Martin Luther King Jr. didn't die in some foolish way. He didn't overdose. He wasn't shot by a jealous lover. He wasn't shot leaving the scene of a crime. He was a man with an earned Ph.D., a Nobel Peace Prize—the youngest to get one at that point; he had oratorical skills off the chart. He could have been a university president or a U.N. ambassador. Yet he died on a balcony in Memphis, Tennessee, helping garbage workers. And they said, "We will shoot this dreamer and see what happens to his dream." And the witness has come to tell you today, to tell you that the dream is still alive! I was born to be a witness.

17.

Just Load the Wagon

Cecil L. "Chip" Murray

IN GEN. 45:17-19 PHARAOH SAYS TO JOSEPH, "Take wagons. Go back to Israel. Bring your children and your wives and your father and come live here in Egypt and live off the fat of the land. Take your wagons." We can all benefit from Pharaoh's words to "just load the wagon."

Many of us remember our mothers or fathers telling us not to worry about the mule being blind, you just load the wagon. Joseph, son of Jacob, has blind faith, so it makes him stubborn as a mule. Normally, it is just the opposite. You and I have blind faith, and it doesn't make us stubborn as a mule. Sometimes it makes us weak as water. God sends us out to a seemingly impossible situation and we go there trembling; instead of trembling with excitement, we tremble with anxiety.

We can learn a lot from the story of the little girl who gets lost in the meadows and a farmer finds her. The farmer tells her not to worry because he'll get her home. With confidence the little girls tells the farmer that she knows he will get her home; she tells him that she had been waiting for him.

"How could you know that I was coming?" he begins to ask the little girl. "When I approached you, all I heard was you reciting the alphabet; you were saying, 'A, B, C, D, E, F, G. . . .'"

"Yes," the girl says. "You see I'm just a little girl, and God knows I'm lost. I didn't know how to ask God, but I did know the letters, so I was just saying the letters, and I figured God could put them together better than I could."

If we would just learn a lesson from this little girl and let God arrange the letter of our lives, we could do anything. If we would just let God arrange the love of our lives and the light of our lives, then even though we walk through the valley of the shadow of death, we can see that light the same way John Newton sees it. He wrote, "I once was lost, but now I am found; I was blind, but now I see." And when you see as Newton saw, when you see as those of us at the Samuel DeWitt Proctor Conference have seen, when you really see, then when God says, "Jump," you just say "How high?"

If God says, "Go," you just say, "When?" If God says, "Now," you just load the wagon and don't worry about the mule being blind. You just load the wagon. The mule belongs to God. The wagon belongs to God. The future belongs to God. The outcome belongs to God. The faith belongs to you and me.

If you have the faith, you can do anything. The substance, the proof, is right there. The evidence is right there. If you just have the faith, God can use you to take nothing and to make something out of it. If you just have the faith, God can get you up off a sickbed and make you as strong as Goliath; if you just have the faith, the Lord will make a way somehow.

Think about the word "providence." It comes from the Latin *providio*, which means ahead and video, or to look. God looks ahead and the Lord will make a way somehow. Don't you worry about the mule being blind. You just load the wagon.

Of course, that little lost child knows that a wagon doesn't move of its own volition. A wagon must have motive power. A wagon can't pull itself, not even a Volkswagen. The Reverend Volkswagen's testimony goes something like this: "I may not be the biggest thing on the road. There are mega-churches, and I just have fifty members. I may not be the baddest thing on the road. I may not be the most beautiful thing on the road, but I want to tell you that the road I'm on is the road that was given to me by God. The road I'm on leads to God. The road I'm on comes from God."

At the midnight hour when the storm is raging, we can learn a lot from that vine. On the safe side of the tree, the vine is at peace. When you've got good health, you ought to say, "Praise the Lord." When you've got some kind of income, you ought to say, "Praise the Lord." When you've got a reason for living, when you've got a ministry in your life, you ought to say, "Praise the Lord." And, if you've got a family, if you've got somebody to love you, you ought to say, "Praise the Lord." On the safe side of the tree, you know that God will take care of the wagon.

But think about the other side of the tree, when the storm of life is raging and the world is tossing me like a ship upon the sea by him who rules the wind and water. As the winds make the vine click or tremble, the vine clings closer to the tree. And so the vine is safe in the midst of the storm.

Perhaps that's where Joseph is caught up—in that storm with his brothers calling him the lord of dreams. And yet he's being told by God, "Don't worry about the mule being blind; just load the wagon." Joseph's brothers call him the lord of dreams because he's a dreamer.

You and I gather at this conference because we are dreamers, and dreamers know what nightmares are. You and I are here because we know that we are in crisis in America. One million two hundred thousand Black men are in prison, locked down. Eighty percent of them are locked up because of substance abuse–related crimes. What we need is prevention more than imprisonment. And the Federal Judicial Council and the Sentencing Project, both out of Washington, D.C., tell us that for a white man to get the same sentence as a Black man for substance abuse, the white man must use a hundred times as much powder cocaine as the Black man uses crack cocaine. However, they are essentially the same substance. A white man gets a 49 percent lower sentencing. A Black man gets a 49 percent higher sentence than a white man for the same crime.

You and I had better be dreamers. We have become consumers instead of producers. We are the ninth richest economy in the world—Black America. We spend 562 billion dollars a year, and the dollar turns over only once in the Black community as compared to five times in the white community and the Latino community, seven times in the Korean community, and twelve to eighteen times in the Jewish community. You and I just spend, spend, spend, and it's gone.

We buy 39 percent of the hair-care products, but Madame C. J. Walker is now gone. We don't own the products. We buy 19 percent of the makeup because we're going to look good, I don't care what you say; we're going to be clean when you see us—but we don't produce it. We buy 25 percent of the Cadillacs sold, yet we don't make the parts. We buy 25 percent of the movie tickets sold. We spend $1,803 on clothing, and we put two dollars in the offering tray.

We have forgotten how to dream. Three-fifths of Americans are overweight and on diets, and the other two-fifths of us should be on diets. We have forgotten how to dream. God speaks to us universally in the form of the Holy Spirit. In every religion in the world, Buddhism, Islam, Judaism, Christianity, Hinduism, there is a Holy Spirit. You and I believe that this Holy Spirit is in this place right now because we can take a hotel and turn it into a sanctuary. We can take an auspicious moment and make it a life-saving moment. The Holy Spirit is in this place, and yet the Holy Spirit speaks to us in terms of dreams. The Holy Spirit speaks to us in the form of dreams. You and I are dreamers.

Joseph, the eleventh son of Jacob, is a dreamer. Joseph, who is the first son of Rachel, the favorite wife of Jacob, is a dreamer. Joseph dreams of standing taller than his brothers. Jacob dreams of standing taller than his peers. You and I would say to Joseph, "Son, be very careful. You don't want to come across as arrogant. The worst thing that could happen to you is to be known as an ego-tripper."

Our pulpits are filled with egos instead of people who are looking to serve the Lord. Our pulpits are filled with people who are filled with themselves instead of being filled with the Holy Spirit. Joseph, you've got to grow up a little. You're going to make your brothers a little insecure.

My brothers and sisters, isn't it about time we grew up? Isn't it about time we learn to work on the problems instead of working on each other? We have the credentials, but can't we see that the greatest credential is when God says, "I send you out from yourself for me"? "I send you out to represent me. Go heal the wounded. Go give sight to the blind. Go give life to the dead."

Isn't it about time you grew up? We've had four hundred years of being grown down, and we have had a history revealed since the 1950s and 1960s. Thank you, Lord, for teaching us our own excellence. Thank you, Lord, for teaching us that we're the oldest people on earth, and DNA proves that we are. There isn't but one race on earth, and that's the Black race. We have other ethnicities, but there is only one race.

Brothers, this is your brother. Why are you jumping on him? There's enough room for everybody. Why don't you lift up your brother? Why are you just calling him a dreamer? Hasn't God given you a dream? Why don't you grow up? Don't you understand that if your situation is not right, God says, "No"? If your time is not right, God says, "Slow." If your growth is not right, God says, "Grow." But when everything is right, God says, "Go." Don't you worry about the mule being blind. You just load the wagon. The mule belongs to God. The wagon belongs to God. The world belongs to God. If God sends you out, just load the wagon.

It can take some time and some trials to grow up. Joseph goes through the night as his own brothers sell him into slavery to the Ishmaelites. And he not only ends up in Egypt, but ends up in jail. Potiphar is one of the government officials in Egypt, and Potiphar's wife really digs on Joseph. I don't want to put women down because the Bible is pretty rough on women. We've got more Potiphars than we have Potiphar wives who get you into trouble. We don't want to blame the sister, but this sister loves Joseph so much that she is almost throwing her pocketbook at him. But Joseph resists the temptation. Joseph is true to his God. So Potiphar's wife prevaricates a little, and Joseph ends up in jail. But, oh, what an awesome God you and I serve!

What we call prison, God calls opportunity. What Shadrach, Meshach, and Abednego call a fire, God calls opportunity. What Daniel calls a lion's den, God calls opportunity. What Jonah calls a whale, God calls opportunity. What you and I call a small parish, God calls opportunity. What you and I call opposition, God calls opportunity.

In Joseph's prison cell comes opportunity. Pharaoh's butler and Pharaoh's baker are in prison, and they meet Joseph and they have dreams. Joseph interprets their dreams, and then later on when Pharaoh has a dream that troubles him, he calls all of his wise men, and none of them can interpret the dream for him. His baker, his butcher, his butler remember this man they met in prison. Pharaoh says, "Bring him here." Joseph interprets the dream. "Your majesty, you're going to have a famine, and here's what you can do to save the people of Egypt." And Pharaoh makes Joseph the number two man in the nation.

You and I see as Joseph walked out of that prison how God can take the prison door off the hinges. You and I see that when things are at their worst, God is at his best. When things are at their worst, God is up to something. When things are down to nothing, God is up to something, and the message is clear. Don't you ever give up! Make them carry you out feet first.

God can take the thing working against you and make it work for you. God can take a negative and turn it into a positive. Look at the beam of the cross that the condemned criminal is required to carry up the hill to Calvary. Jesus is so physically debilitated that he has to have another person, Simeon, a Black man from North Africa, carry the cross. And when Simeon reaches down and makes eye contact with Jesus, something wonderful happens. He helps him carry his negativity up the hill of Calvary. And waiting on the hill is the vertical post like a vertical intrusion from heaven above. Here is eternity waiting. And when time and eternity are wed—where Jesus lays his head at the intersection of time and eternity—you and I are born. That's where the wagon gets its motive power. That's where we can say, "Don't you worry about the mule being blind; you just load the wagon. The Lord will make a way somehow."

And in gratitude for Joseph's saving Egypt, Pharaoh says, "Take wagons. Go back home, get your wives, get your children, get your father, come here and live off of the fat of the land." Joseph does that, and that's where we leave them right now—there in the palace hugging and kissing and weeping and making up. And the brothers of Joseph apologize. They say, "We're sorry, Joseph. If we just had it to do over again, we'd never make that mistake again. You should be so angry at us that you could be putting us to death, but here you are feeding us, and not only feeding us but feeding us richly." And forgiving Joseph says, "That's all right—you meant it for evil, but God meant it for good."

That's alright. The Lord will make a way somehow. That's alright, you're not my enemy; you are my family. So what do you and I have to conclude? No longer can we sing: "Go down, Moses, way down in Egypt land. Tell old Pharaoh to let my people go." Pharaoh is not our enemy. We do not have to tell Pharaoh to let my people go, but we have to tell my people to let my people go! Our problem is not with Pharaoh but with "Negro." There's plenty good room on the wagon, Negro. There's plenty good room on the wagon. Don't you worry about the wagon. Don't you worry about the mule. Don't you worry about the mule being blind; just load the wagon in the name of Jesus!

18.

Black Church Leadership in the Age of AIDS

What Must We Do to Be Saved?

Transcribed and edited from a plenary address delivered by Monifa A. Jumanne

MY WORK IN THE FIELD OF FAITH-BASED HIV PREVENTION at the Interdenominational Theological Center (ITC) is informed by a lifetime of social justice activism and a commitment to faith as liberating praxis. Like many of you, I subscribe to liberation theology. If Jesus was not a liberator, what was he? I believe that the indomitable faith of our African ancestors shaped our past, frames our present and will ensure our future. Therefore, my message today is one of faith and hope. As Kelly Brown Douglas says in the introduction to her book, *Sexuality and the Black Church*, I, too, "am compelled to do my best, to contribute as boldly as I can to the Black struggle for life and wholeness."[1] So I offer these brief comments about HIV/AIDS and African Americans with three questions in mind: Do we want to be healed? Whom shall we send? And what must we do to be saved?

We can confidently locate the issues of HIV/AIDS within the context of the Black church, for every African American community of faith—regardless of denomination or tradition—has been touched by HIV and AIDS in some way. But it would be a gross misuse of contextual analysis and a deliberate exercise in ethnic self-delusion to examine such issues without insisting upon the genuine interests, intent, and interaction of Black people themselves. For whether we are addressing the efforts to treat AIDS, the attempts to contain

AIDS, or the struggle to prevent AIDS, we are speaking *to* ourselves, *about* ourselves and in this venue, *for* ourselves.

The need to define ourselves and our struggle is necessary in order to set the captives free. This need is reflected in Ralph Ellison's literary classic, *Invisible Man*. Whether you read this novel as a coming-of-age story, an individual quest for identity, or a powerful indictment of the absurdity of racism, the story remains today fresh and relevant. Ellison speaks to the individual and collective need for African Americans to acquire self-knowledge, self-definition, and self-illumination. He beckons us to become visible to ourselves. This is not just a national problem; it is global, as well. And it is—whether we like it or not—an individual problem. The dichotomy for us is that we must engage the issue at the level of national and international genocide—although many think that this is not genocide—and we must engage the issues as they affect our everyday lives. The issues affect the way we have sex, the way we talk to our children about physical intimacy, the way we look at ourselves, and the way we express our sexuality.

Frederick William Faber's enduring hymn *Faith of Our Fathers* mirrors the admonishment given in Jude 1:3: "contend for the faith that was once for all entrusted to the saints." Likewise, A. B. Patton's contemporary rendition, *Faith of Our Mothers*, illustrates 2 Tim. 1:5 in a way that waxes more melancholic, but is no less determined. He says, "I am reminded of your sincere faith, a faith that lived first in your grandmother Lois and your mother Eunice." These songs speak of living faith, lavish faith, guiding faith, Christian faith, and faith in God's faithfulness that is the cornerstone of Christendom. Yet faith as we knew it and know it now in the postmodern world is at a critical crossroad. In fact, in the court of world opinion, faith is on trial. Some judges have already dismissed the case, while others have ruled insufficient evidence. Today, even among African Americans—a historically religious and spiritual people—the concept of faith has been dressed up, watered down, deconstructed, and reconstructed into a toothless lion with a small roar and an even smaller bite. Everywhere in the world the role of and need for faith have been challenged. As a result, our churches have been inundated with a smokescreen of programs that are faith-placed, but not faith-based.

Nowhere is this issue regarding the role of faith more glaringly evident than in the global pandemic of HIV/AIDS. In a mere twenty-three years, AIDS has metamorphosed from a disease of gay white men, which it never actually was, into what former U.S. Surgeon General David Satcher referred to as increasingly a disease of people of color. The question we have to stop and ask ourselves every time we hear that is, Why? Are African Americans genetically predisposed to social pathology? Is this virus somehow able to surreptitiously discern the vulnerable zones in our communities and then exhaust its toxic venom before it migrates to others? If race and ethnicity are not risk factors for HIV and AIDS—and the federal government assures us that they are not—why then is there such a disproportionate incidence of AIDS among African Americans? Are African Americans engaging in *more* risky sexual activity or doing *more* drugs than any other population? Could it be that the agencies that are providing the money to "fight AIDS" are the very agencies that are promoting its existence?

One thing is certain: our ability to extract the most accurate answer is impeded by our inability to ask the right questions. Too many of us have become comfortable sleeping with the enemy. We have dug in our heels for the long haul, as if AIDS is our own personal ethnic pathology. Our leaders have stopped asking about the conspiracy theory or the genocidal threat. Yet these same leaders are devoting significant portions of their often meager resources to fight an enemy whose presence is still a mystery and whose departure from our community is not even a topic of polite conversation.

Keep two things in mind: AIDS is not accidental, and AIDS is not ours. Some have called it a weapon of mass destruction. Since June 1981, when the Centers for Disease Control and Prevention (CDC) formally identified this incurable disease, many aspects of the HIV/AIDS phenomenon have changed. Geography, economics, gender, age, and color have changed. But two key factors have not changed: how HIV is spread and how HIV is prevented. When an enemy is this silent, this pervasive, this invisible, and this treacherous, we have to use its own tactics against it. We have to fight fire with fire…and faith. In other words, if we know that a particular behavior is going to spread the virus, then we should avoid engaging in that behavior. Think about it—we do not actually prevent HIV; we prevent the *behaviors* that spread HIV. The best protection is still prevention. And the best prevention is a relationship with a God whose power can keep us away from the behaviors that spread HIV. And while that may be a challenge for some, the prevalence of the virus and the absence of a cure should compel us to refrain from dismissing *avoidance of risk* as a goal too difficult to achieve. So the first question is critically important: Do we want to be healed?

Our reference point here is not solely the United States, for the motherland is being dismantled before our eyes. The land is changing hands—again. The diamonds, the gold, the copper, the silicon, the latex, the rubber, the oil, are changing hands—again. How?

Approximately 95 percent of people living with HIV and AIDS live in so-called developing countries (Will they ever be developed?). Sub-Saharan Africa is the hardest-hit region. Why? If you look at a world map with Africa in the center, the 95 percent is right there. Nine hundred thousand—maybe a million—of the cases are in the United States, 0.5 percent in Central Europe, but 95 percent in Africa. This could not possibly be an accident. You can read these statistics on anybody's Web site, but remember that statistics belie the multiple epidemics of oppression, repression, and depression that restrict the freedom of Africans to know or have access to life beyond this very real danger.

Statistics—mere numbers on a page—conceal the millions of children sitting in classrooms waiting for a teacher who died last night. Numbers conceal the millions of women who insisted on condom use by their philandering boyfriends and husbands—women who were subsequently beaten, burned, or abandoned. Numbers don't show the acres of farmland that have now become acres of graveyards, or the pastors who conduct more funerals than worship services and who wear clergy vestments day and night because, for them, there is no day off from death. Numbers do not silence the cries of dying babies—languishing in garbage dumps where their frightened and destitute parents have left them.

In his *Letters and Papers from Prison*, theologian Dietrich Bonhoeffer asked, "Are we still of any use?"[2] For academicians, theologians, pastors, and researchers, this is a relevant question, for Bonhoeffer noted, "What we need is not geniuses or cynics or even clever tacticians, but just plain, honest, straightforward people." Plain, honest people will not only question the role of God's people in administering care and compassion to persons infected and affected by HIV/AIDS (If you call yourself a Christian, ministering to someone who is sick is a given, not an option. Jesus never asked, "What does he/she have?" before visiting the sick.), they will also question the origin of AIDS and its ubiquitous presence among African Americans.

With the vengeance of a California forest fire, AIDS has swept across the amber waves of grain and purple mountain majesty of America, strategically passing over other people's doorposts and wedging itself into a permanent position in African American life. African Americans neither manufactured HIV nor imported it into Black neighborhoods, yet we are the ones who have to do the work of getting it out—like all the other pathologies. Now we need an answer to the second question: "Whom shall we send?"

Are we waiting for the government to rescue us from this still-suspicious malady, or are we willing to rescue—to send—ourselves?

A teacher once spent weeks reading Anansi the Spider stories to her fifth grade class. One little boy appeared deeply disturbed each time a story concluded and the clever spider had once again outsmarted the lion. After all, the lion was the king of the jungle. Very troubled, the child asked his teacher, "When will the lion win?" The teacher answered quickly, "When the lion writes the story."

We have to write our own story. When we write the story, we will not conceptualize AIDS as an entity unto itself, because the issue is much larger than the disease. Think, as the saying goes, outside the box. What may be needed at this point is a reframing of the problem. Think about it: a well-organized, white, gay community, whose point of cohesion is sympathy, drives 80-90 percent of the national response to HIV/AIDS. What is our point of cohesion? Is it sympathy, outrage, compassion, fatalism, or accountability? Is it all that and more? The problem here is that we have grown content letting someone else set our part of the AIDS agenda, and we can't own it the way they define it. When we write the story, we're going to get past merely being sympathetic. When we write the story, we're going to get past sexuality. When we write the story, we are going to get past ourselves, and get to God, where we were in the first place before we began, perhaps inadvertently, to sabotage our own future.

And let's give credit where credit is due: The Black church *is* involved in preventing HIV, fighting AIDS, and providing AIDS-related services. ITC and its counterpart organizations have conducted too many faith-based HIV prevention programs for us to still be playing that tape. In confronting the tough issues of drugs, prostitution and sexuality in his book, *Another Day's Journey*, Robert Franklin presented results from a study of Black clergy at the Hampton University Ministers Conference. On the issue of sexuality, almost 80 percent of those ministers said that they had taught about and preached several sermons on the issue of sexuality. 85 percent had preached against premarital sex. But 34 percent thought AIDS was a divine curse.[3] Let's set the record straight: AIDS is neither a curse nor a blessing. It is a *consequence* of somebody's behavior. The "A" in AIDS stands for acquired, which means you have to do something (or someone must do something to you) to contract it. Franklin calls for increased education about sexuality and disease transmission so that clergy and congregations do not inflict greater pain on the lives of people who are suffering and searching for empathy and care. After all, the job of the shepherd is not only to lead the flock out of harm's way, but also to empower the flock to lead itself out of harm's way.

In 1 Sam. 17 Saul and the armies of Israel gathered in the Valley of Elah and held their breath as a crazy young shepherd boy named David ran onto a Philistine battlefield to confront a nine-foot, uncircumcised giant named Goliath. Despite seemingly overwhelming odds, David's unwavering faith in God equipped him to defeat this pompous enemy. Today, HIV/AIDS is an arrogant Goliath parading triumphantly on the battlefield of African American communities. We are not afraid of giants. God is on our side. Faith is on our side. Which brings us to the final question: What must we do to be saved?

How much are we willing to sacrifice to slay this giant, to curb this epidemic among ourselves? No, we did not bring AIDS into our communities, but we have to get rid of it. Are we depending on the CDC or on Health and Human Services to save us? The truth is that all the federal dollars in the world will not save us if we are not willing to save ourselves. While it is sometimes true that our people are destroyed for lack of knowledge, it is also true that our people are destroyed because God has given us knowledge that we choose, for whatever reason, not to use.

Having knowledge and using knowledge are too often mutually exclusive endeavors. Some of us are looking for ways to "sin" more effectively, as in Huey Lewis's lyrics from the 1980s: "I want a new drug, one that won't make me sick." We want to keep engaging in risky behavior; we just don't want to get infected. We can't ignore the direct connection between what we sow and what we reap. In *The Inward Journey* Howard Thurmond admonishes: Do your own thinking. In fact, Thurmond says, knowledge affects a person's pride and arrogance, but wisdom makes for understanding and humility.[4] Wisdom calls for a theology of prevention. If you have a congregation of two thousand people, and one hundred of them (that you know of) are infected, you have 1,900 people to keep from moving over to the infected side. It makes sense to put your efforts into prevention of HIV, while you treat, care for, and minister to persons who are already sick.

At Tavis Smiley's State of the Black Church gala last year in Detroit, Rev. Dr. Jeremiah Wright suggested that African Americans need to turn off the cameras, shut the doors, and begin to do some serious soul-searching and solution generating among ourselves. I concur. This is not about form or fashion; it is about what we must do to be saved. To be saved, we cannot allow our existence to be defined by a problem, nor can we afford the luxury of subscribing to a grant mentality, so that when the grant is over, so is the work. To be saved, we cannot allow our brothers and sisters to be discarded, discounted and dismissed. Every person who enters our churches or our places of worship should be welcomed, respected, and valued. After all, the person with HIV or AIDS may look like he or she is desperate, but the person in the BMW, the Armani suit, and the upscale subdivision, may be even more desperate.

So our focus should not just be on AIDS but on our ability to move beyond it. We have some good stuff going for us, but we need strategies with long-term viability. We cannot throw out the baby with the bathwater. To save ourselves, we must re-examine our own strengths as a people: our historical resilience, our cultural self-determination, and our old-fashioned attitudes toward responsible sexual behavior. Reaffirming our faith in God is a good starting point. Putting an end to child molestation, incest, rape, and domestic violence is a good follow-up. Engaging in a respectful discourse on sexuality is another viable strategy. Ultimately, the war against HIV/AIDS is one that neither the Black Church nor the Black community can win alone. Together, however, we have what it takes to save ourselves. We people of faith can take the battlefield as David did: shrewd, smart, and spiritually armed not just to confront, but to defeat, this modern-day Goliath.

Let me close with a story. A young Jewish student sought to repay his teacher for a hurt that he had endured. It seemed that the rabbi had said something in a previous lecture that the student had found humiliating, and, instead of discussing it, the student intended to humiliate the rabbi in front of the class. The student held his closed hands behind his back and said, "Rabbi, I have bird in my hand. Is it alive or dead?" Had the Rabbi answered "alive," the young man would have crushed the bird in his hand and brought out its lifeless body. Had the professor said "dead," the student would have brought his hand forward and released the bird into the lofty chambers of the lecture hall. The rabbi was a very wise and gentle man. After considering both the student's motive and his question, he responded, "The answer, my son, is in your hands."

Yes, faith is under attack, but faith is the best we have, faith in God's ability to do what God does best—redeem, deliver, heal, transform, restore, and sustain. Reexamine the ending to 1 Sam. 17. Goliath loses. I submit to all of us today that the answer to the scourge of HIV/AIDS among us, our people, our community, our future, is in our hands.

19.

At the Table

The Next Generation

Portia Wills Lee, Otis Moss III, Stacey L. Edwards, and Reginald Williams

THE FOLLOWING FOUR SERMONS are from young leaders in ministry; they share their thoughts on how we need to reach the next generation and present models for blowing the trumpet in Zion.

What Happens When a People Loses the Capacity to Dream?

Portia Wills Lee

In order to effectively sound the trumpet in Zion, we have to continue dreaming, no matter where we are in life, and encourage all people to do the same. No matter what stage we are in life, we should always continue to dream. Dreams mean that we are keeping hope alive. Dreaming means that we understand the story.

In her book *Listening for God* Rev. Dr. Renita Weems states, "Often when I lose my way I rely on stories to get me through the deafening silence."[1] In a culture in which there is an intergenerational disconnection; in a culture in which there is hip-hop, gangsta rap; in a culture in which big enough is not enough, microwave is not fast enough; in a culture in which parents are rushing their children off to violin, piano, and acting classes; in a society in which we rush our children to football, soccer, tennis, and golf lessons—when do we have time to tell the stories so that our children will understand that the dreaming is in the story?

We are in an intergenerational disconnect. Even in our churches, where we have youth Bible studies and we have youth Sunday school classes and we have youth ministries and we even have youth worship services, how do we establish a paradigm that will create an intergenerational movement that allows the seasoned ones to simply tell their dream stories that kept them moving at a time when they were told they couldn't dream? We must become intergenerationally connected so the stories can pass on.

You see, I'm a propounding pastor, but often in pastoring a church I have found I have relied upon the stories that Dr. Cynthia Hale shared with me. And when the darkness becomes so gloomy, when I can't see my way out—I think back on the stories Dr. Hale shared with me. When I can't see any hope and it seems as if all hope is gone, I rely on the stories that I heard from Dr. Barbara King, and I can look and see from whence God has brought her, and it gives me hope.

But if we don't tell our children the story—if we just allow them to think that it's okay to want prosperity and not to understand that on one hand there is a struggle, but on the other hand there is a story of victory—what will happen? I'm so thankful that I grew up on a block where there were not very many children. For entertainment I would have to visit the neighborhood elders. I just loved going to visit Mrs. Katie in her front yard as she tended her roses. I would hear her talk about the stories of working for a "decent" white family. She would go on to stress that they could not take away her dignity because she had the story of a God who gave her dignity.

I was so blessed to know the story of an elder and Mrs. Couch, who didn't have to talk; they walked the walk of a loving God and simply loved God's people. And then I would go on down two houses, and I was blessed to know Mr. and Mrs. Watkins. Do you see what I'm saying? God is trying to tell us something. Can you hear God speaking through the stories? Mr. Watkins would say, "Daughter, always dream. Always be a dreamer." He'd go on to emphasize the importance of having a good education, and then he'd say how important it is to know how to save a little money on the side.

I recently read about Donald Watkins, reportedly the first Black billionaire in this country. His grandfather was the same Mr. Watkins who preached to me about dreaming. He stressed that his grandfather always taught him to have good work ethics and the wisdom of financial investment. All the stories—that's what empowers us to be the people of God.

My favorite story was from an old woman who lived across the street. She was a dreamer in a society that said she couldn't dream.

Her mother told her, "You can't be no preacher woman." Her mother said, "You don't need to be a missionary." Her mother simply said to go to college, learn to teach our people, and "get yourself a husband." But Mrs. Qualls told me that she never stopped dreaming. She satisfied her mother, but she kept on dreaming. And she shared with me, "Baby girl, when they said I couldn't preach, I just simply went to the prison, and I preached to the inmates."

Don't ever stop dreaming. And because Mrs. Qualls taught this baby girl how to dream, I'm still dreaming today. Old Mrs. Qualls is 105 years old today. She doesn't know when Sunday comes anymore. She doesn't remember that she used to go to the jail. But when the days are rough, I can still look at her—a woman who taught three generations in my family—and because she dreamed at a time when women weren't supposed to dream, I think about Mrs. Qualls who simply said, When they close one door on you, you'd better know that if you're a dreamer, God will open another door. When I think back on the stories, I have to give God some praise, and I look for a way to tell another generation simple stories that my elders passed on to me.

But today within our Black church structure, within our bourgeois Negro society, the challenge becomes: How do we pass on the stories when nobody wants to know the stories of how far God has brought us? We've got to be creative. You see, our children have to know the stories. The youth must know the stories. We must connect them to another generation. The scripture says we are commanded to tell the stories.

What did the Israelites do? God said that when they crossed over the river, they placed some stones there. God said, When your children ask in generations to come, "What do these stones mean?" you'd better tell the stories. You've got to find a way to be creative in merging the stories together. We've got to allow an opportunity within our church settings—not only for the elders—but for the drug addicts in a crack-infected society to come in and tell their stories.

I had the audacity—because I am a dreamer—to bring in the crack addicts. In a little church we need every member we can get. Not everyone liked it; I had some folks saying, "I don't want my children sitting next to a crack addict or a former prostitute," and they left the church. But my ten-year-old daughter simply said to me, "Mommy, what's going to happen one day when their children might decide to use some drugs and they don't know the story of that crack addict? You see, Mommy, I don't want no drugs because I see what the crack addict is talking about when they just merely stand up and give a testimony about trying to find God in the midst of their addiction. Oh, Mommy, I don't want drugs." (That's the wisdom of a child.)

I tell those who want to be prophetic to tell the stories. God is speaking. Can you hear me now? God is trying to ask us, Can you hear me in the story? There are prisoners out there, elderly prisoners who've been incarcerated most of their lives. You'd better allow them to come in and tell you stories because if they don't tell them, we're going to have more men and women incarcerated. Don't think that we have arrived! We will arrive if we continue simply to tell the stories.

Discerning among Theologies in the Black Church
Otis Moss III

We have three prevalent theologies in the Black church today: a theology of pimps, a theology of prostitutes, and a theology of prophets. Unfortunately, some of us are unable to discern among theologies. In order to be a prophetic witness to the oppressed, we must make sure that we do not have a ministry of self but a ministry that is committed to the community. To evaluate our ministries, let us consider two paradigms: our temples and our theologies.

As for our temples, we are in the age of the Solomon tabernacle. It is a tabernacle that does not move. It stays in one place, and there can be a tendency—especially with middle-class bourgeois theology—to deify the house we are in and not recognize that it is God who has established the house. And so, for those of us who come into certain ministries where the house has already been established, there are always Pharisees already in place who want us to worship the house but not the One who made the house.

When we look at the Mosaic narrative, we recognize that the tabernacle was mobile. It never stayed in one place because God never stays in one place. Therefore, if we have a theological framework from the Mosaic narrative, then we understand that culture does change and methodologies change, but God stays the same. Whenever we get stuck in looking at the world and the ministry from a Solomon temple perspective, we will end up in a position where we are unable to do the work and the will of God.

Since we are out of the Christian tradition, Jesus is a wedge between the Solomon tradition and the Mosaic tradition because he is the temple and he is also mobile in his ministry and recognizes that wherever he goes, God is there. If we follow Jesus, we bring together two narratives. Since we understand that God has been placed in us, wherever we go is the temple of God. And so, wherever we lay down roots, we are then able to lift up the Word and the power of God wherever we go. So those become the two paradigms of worship for this generation.

As for theology, I believe—and I received some of this belief from my father—that we have three levels of theology that are pervasive in our community. There is a "pimp theology," which raises this question: What can you do for me? That's the fundamental question that every pimp wants to know. And many of us become seduced—sometimes unintentionally—by pimp theology. Some of us are coming into situations our parents could never have dreamed of. We come into a church that has three thousand people, and you have a staff and all of this, and because you want to protect what you have, you end up allowing the pimp theology to move into your spirit.

Or it may be that some of us are seduced by a prosperity gospel, which then focuses on the residue of the blessings of God instead of the actual blessings of God. If we were to translate one of the words for blessing in the Old Testament, it literally means the shoulder of God. In other words, blessing means to be near the presence and power of God. And my grandmother, who has gone on to be with the Lord, explained this to me in a unique way. She used to make something called tea cakes. When she would make the tea cakes, this is what she would do. She would say, "Otis, come here." She would pour the tea cakes into the pan, and there was always a residue left over in her bowl. And she would say, "Otis, you can lick the residue, but don't eat too much of the residue because the real blessing is in the oven." And a lot of the theology we have today is residue theology, in which we are focused on houses, cars, clothes—that's nothing but residue. The real power is the power and the presence of God. That is the blessing, because you can take the house, you can take the car, you can take the job, but if I have God in my life, I am still blessed.

Sojourner Truth was blessed, but she didn't have a Bentley. Harriet Tubman didn't have a great house, but she was blessed because she had the power and the presence of the Most High God.

Another kind of theology involves prostituting the gospel. Because the prostitute says, "What can I do for you?" And this happens when we come into a rural situation in which the pastor does everything and becomes a kind of prostitute to the congregation, and all the pastor wants is to do everything for the congregation but not to do anything for his or her own family. So pastors in that situation end up with a divided narrative in terms of their life, in which they are great leaders but terrible parents. And so we have to deal with the prostitute theology and narrative that are now operating within our community.

What we really need today is a prophetic theology. The prophet does not say, "What can you do for me?" The prophet says, "What can we do together?" And that is the prophetic narrative that we are seeking in this day and age, and it only comes when we are familiar and know the word intimately and have elders in our midst who are able to teach us like Dr. Jeremiah A. Wright Jr. and Dr. Iva Carruthers, elders who are able to pass on those great stories like Rev. Samuel Kyles.

When I was about twelve years old, I went to rent this movie called *The Guns of Navarone*, starring Gregory Peck. Neither my mom, nor dad, nor I had ever seen the movie. When the movie was about to end, it didn't look like Gregory Peck was going to get out of the situation, and I was upset. And, my mother was upset. But my father was calm; he was cool, and he was collected. As the film was wrapping up, my mother started pacing the floor, I started holding on to my seat, and my dad was just chilling. I could not understand it, so I said to my father, "Why is it that you're so cool about everything? Don't you know Gregory is going to die? Have you seen this movie before?" He said, "No, I haven't seen the movie, but I did read the book."

If we know the book and we know the story, we know, "If God be for us, then who can be against us?" It's good to know the theologians, but also know the Bible. It's good to know Toni Morrison and Zora Neale Hurston, but make sure you know the Book. Because if you know the Book, you'll know that "no weapon formed against us shall prosper." If you know the Book, you know that "the Lord is my light and my salvation, whom shall I fear?" If you know the Book, you know that God will never leave you nor forsake you. Make sure that whatever you do in ministry, you read the Book!

What Does the Incarnational Presence of God Look like in These Times?

Stacey L. Edwards

As ministers moving into the twenty-first century, it is pertinent that we become an incarnational presence. We are the one just as Christ was the One. He came into the world so that we might recognize that we are the ones to liberate our people. And how does this incarnational presence look in our ministry to the oppressed? I offer two examples from our ministries at Trinity United Church of Christ in

Chicago: a Friday lunchtime worship service in the historic Chicago loop and a singles' ministry that addresses the holistic needs of the community.

Ever since the inception of "F. A.T. Fridays" in September 2003, hundreds of people—including professionals and nonprofessionals, members of Trinity and nonmembers of Trinity, churched and unchurched—have ceased their daily business and taken their valuable time and their personal lunch breaks to worship the Lord. In the heart of Chicago's legendary Loop, many people have chosen to praise and thank the Lord during F. A.T. Fridays, which means "Feasting at the Throne" on Fridays.

F. A.T. Friday is simply a taste of Trinity United Church of Christ in the Loop. It is situated in downtown Chicago, commencing at high noon and concluding at 12:45 p.m. F. A.T. Friday is a complete worship service that gives workers an opportunity to relax, relate, release, and rejoice in a space that is nonthreatening, empowering, and enlightening. And people can return to their offices within sixty minutes.

F. A.T. Friday is a response to the heightened corporate greed and economic dismay we experience. F. A.T. Friday incorporates the convenience and technology that our society is accustomed to while addressing relevant issues such as unemployment, racism, social injustice, get-rich-quick schemes, and the chaotic lifestyles too many of us live. The sacred time on Fridays is also designed to help African Americans who feel disconnected get connected with other Black folks in the downtown area. Therefore, as an alternative to an escape via a bar or a club or other venue, F. A.T. Friday is designed to equip God's people in faith so that they might be better able to deal with the frustrations of their workweek as well as the local, national, international, and family and personal problems that impede their daily lives.

F. A.T. Friday worship meshes the head and the heart. It combines the spiritual and the social and the political. It connects the public to the prophetic voice of justice, light, and love from God. It is equivalent to Emmanuel because it reminds workers that God is with them—not only in the church place but also in the workplace.

F. A.T. Friday is a respite and a holistic worship service. It is a substantial, meaningful, targeted, intentional, and relevant expression of ministry that reaches beyond the walls of the church and meets people where they are at their point of need—all in forty-five minutes. For twelve minutes we praise and worship; for three minutes we celebrate through a call to worship; for two minutes we welcome everyone and share announcements; for seven minutes we lift an offering and sing. For seven minutes we have teaching and preaching a sermon, and in three minutes we extend an invitation to accept Christ and give the benediction. By 12:45 individuals walk out of the building with a free, healthy brown-bag lunch and return to the office.

F.A.T. Fridays also turned into a public relations tool. The service shares what Trinity is, who Trinity is, and what Trinity is about. As a result, people have joined our church.

Since its inception F.A.T. Fridays has grown in quality and quantity. We have also noticed that a lot of the people were coming for prayer to release their burdens. As a result of this observation, we are adding a new component to Fridays. We're dreaming again, but we know that within the next six months God is going to open up a space downtown, and we will be providing counseling for workers in the Chicago Loop.

Incarnational ministry realizes that church does not only happen on Sunday. Church isn't just four walls that enclose us on Sunday mornings. Each of us—we are the church. Church is a way of life. It is a way of being. It is the way we interact. It's community. We are going to have to be the church every day so that we might meet the people where they are and draw people into a closer relationship with God.

Our singles' community has also emerged as a model for incarnational ministry. We merged the single adult ministry with the single parent ministry within our church to address the needs of one of the largest constituents of the church—singles. Unfortunately, there are many negative connotations that come with being single. People think that to be single means to be deficient, half, or less. But to be single actually means to be unique and to be whole. And I want to be unique and whole, whether I'm married or I'm single.

Therefore, the first thing the singles community seeks to do is redefine what singleness is. Because once people can become comfortable in their uniqueness and their wholeness in God, they will begin living a different type of reality. So we have the singles community, and within the singles community we have different families. If you help people realize that they are a part of community, they will begin acting and living like they are in a community. Within the singles community we have never-married families, single parents, divorced people, widows, forty years old and over, and so forth. We also have unmarried couples—people who are in dating relationships. Within the Black community a major problem is that many of us do not have models for marriage, so within the singles community we also help people enhance their relationships and move toward marriage.

Within the life of the community we also have a same-gender-loving family. We are openly affirming same-gender-loving people. What is same-gender loving? It is homosexual, gay, lesbian, bisexual, and transgender loving. Within our ministry people know that no matter if they are female or male or same-gender-loving or heterosexual they will be affirmed in God to be the people who God has created them to be—not who I told them to be, because I didn't create them. People are encouraged to be the people who God has called them to be. And as a result, our ministry has added nearly three hundred people. Because the place was affirming, it was not victimizing. We have to create safe spaces for people to come and be who they are in God and to partner in ministry so that they can be who God has created them to be.

Finally, I would like to suggest that if we are going to help people live out God's purpose in their lives, we are going to have to be an incarnational presence and to create spaces that are safe, that are not victimizing, that are not judgmental, that are not condemning. John 3:16-17 reminds us: For God so loved the world. . . . Dr. Gardner C. Taylor reminds us of the word "whosoever" in this text. God so loved the world that "whosoever" believes in him shall not perish but have everlasting life. And the Christ came into the world not to condemn the world but through him, through the life that he lived, that all the world might be saved.

Now What? Where Do We Go from Here?

Reginald Williams

As we reflect on what our eyes and ears have experienced, and how the internal infernos of our collective souls have been enflamed, we must pause and ask the question: Now what?

Throughout this historic conference, we have heard the what and the why, and in this moment of sending forth, I want to suggest a how. I want to suggest Trinity United Church of Christ's Justice Ministry as a model of ministry that is internally based and externally relevant.

At Trinity we have a justice division within our Christian Education Ministry. The justice division is comprised of ministries that serve the people who need the services of the ministry. These ministries also track the progression of issues that are directly related to the ministry area of concern.

For example, our HIV/AIDS ministry helps people who are living with HIV/AIDS to cope with the myriad of concerns that come with living with this disease. The ministry provides continuous testing and care for the soul of persons who are infected. Safe space is provided in an anonymous location for persons to pray, commune, and be counseled on their condition and the proper way to care for themselves. This is care for the soul of the person living with the disease. However, the other purpose of the ministry is to keep the congregation aware of legislation and political action that take place related to the issue of HIV/AIDS. This is the educational component of the ministry. And out of this educational component come actions. When you know better, you can do better. Letters can be written, boycotts can be staged, and action can take place to help change some of the conditions that we face.

Another example of an internally based and externally relevant ministry is the housing ministry. The mission and charge of our housing ministry is to help educate persons about home ownership and all that home ownership encompasses. The housing ministry also helps those looking for affordable rental housing and those in emergency situations, such as families whose homes have been burned or families who have been kicked out or who are homeless. This is the ministry to the concern and care of the soul of the person and family. The other part of the ministry is to watch the landscape of the political scene with regard to housing. In Chicago over the past few years public housing has been torn down. In place of the public housing that has been destroyed, plans are being made to build one-, two-, and three-hundred-thousand-dollar homes. Persons displaced from public housing have nowhere to go. Vouchers do not count for much, especially now that President George W. Bush is knocking even more money off of housing vouchers. And the cost of living in Chicago is extremely high. A family of three making approximately seven dollars an hour has to work about 140 hours per week just to afford the average two-bedroom apartment in Chicago. Armed with this information, we joined in with other concerned clergy and parishes throughout the city to write and tell the city council to do something about the exorbitant costs in the city.

Justice ministries in the Black church should not be the same as an organizing campaign, although they can benefit from the principles of organizing. Justice ministries must serve the parishioner in need as well as fight for proper policies in the relevant area of concern.

Within the division of justice at Trinity the focus is on collaboration among the justice ministries. In other words, the push and the urge are for ministries to collaborate on various projects and ministry opportunities. In all of our churches we know that only a few folks do most of the work. Therefore, the push for collaboration takes the load off of the same five saints who always do the grunt work every time the ministries meet. Collaborations make ministry more efficient, effective, and holistic as the various ministries bring their own expertise to the ministry opportunity.

For example, in 2004 the ward in which our church sits was set to receive the year's highest number of persons released from prison in the city. Therefore, members of our prison ministry have come up with an idea for an aftercare program. This aftercare program aims to be a one-stop shop where ex-offenders can obtain assistance with job skills from our career development ministry, possible housing options from our housing ministry, legal assistance from our legal counseling ministry, and health counseling from our health and wellness ministry. This is one model of ministry for justice ministries within the church.

In another example of church collaboration we are in the nascent stages of developing a coalition of churches that reach across denominational lines to work on social justice issues together. Some ministers' coalitions have prayer breakfasts and worship services together, but we wanted this coalition to specifically deal with church collaborations on justice issues. This is our only purpose. All of our parishioners, regardless of denomination, are subject to the ills of this society and the policies of local, state, and federal governments. All of us and our parishioners are subject to walking while Black, breathing while Black, driving while Black, and learning while Black. When police brutality occurs, the officer does not ask what church you attend or your denominational affiliation. Since adverse policies reach across denominational lines, why can't we reach across those same lines to do something about those same policies? With this in mind we have brought together United Methodist, Swedish Covenant, United Church of Christ, and Roman Catholic pastors of congregations to work on issues together. We sat down in a room and thought through the most important issues that affect all of our congregations. We came up with eight major long-term issues and decided to work on the three that were the most important and imminent: voter education, workers' rights, and the pandemic of HIV/AIDS.

Our model consists of interdenominational collaboration on shared concerns and issues. We may not agree on all things, but there are some things we can agree on. We may not agree on all things, but disagreements don't break up the family, nor do disagreements stop the family from working together. The prophetic work of Jesus and Isaiah must be the center of our movement—to liberate the oppressed, open blinded eyes, and proclaim the favorable year of the Lord.

One of the areas we are working on around workers' rights involves the largest corporation in the world, Wal-Mart, which has net profits of more than $245 billion. But while the firm is a huge success in terms of business growth and profits, it engages in some very troubling practices. Employees and the U.S. Equal Employment Opportunity Commission have won a number of lawsuits against Wal-Mart, charging discrimination on the basis of gender, race, ethnicity, and disability. Additional suits are pending. In December 2002 a jury in Portland, Oregon found that Wal-Mart engaged in widespread and unwavering violations of U.S. laws in forcing employees to work unpaid overtime. According to the case, some workers who clocked out after forty hours of work were pressured by their managers to work off the clock without pay. This is just one of thirty-five suits in thirty states that are filed and awaiting trial. Sound familiar? Sounds like plantation work.

One of the reasons for Wal-Mart's success is its low prices. Its low prices are explained in part by the low wages paid to its workers. In 2001 sales clerks at Wal-Mart were paid an average of $8.23 per hour and had annual earnings of less than $14,000 per year. This is too little to keep a family of three out of poverty. Union workers in grocery stores are paid approximately $1.20 more than Wal-Mart workers and are roughly twice as likely to have employer-sponsored health care and be offered a pension. I want to be clear about this. Wal-Mart does not provide health care to its full-time, hourly employees until they have worked there for six months. Part-time workers cannot get health care until year two. And when they offer you the health care plan, it costs so much (from this company that makes $245 billion a year) that many of the workers are only able to take home pennies out of their paychecks. Therefore, they cannot really afford to get sick. In October 2003, in a raid of Wal-Mart stores in twenty-one states, federal agents found janitors who had been forced to work every day for eight months without a single day off. These workers were not employed by Wal-Mart directly but by a firm contracting with Wal-Mart.

Within this framework Wal-Mart is now making a move from suburbs to cities. This is the case in Chicago. If what is done in the suburbs is done in the cities, then the small-business community will be wiped out. And if Wal-Mart does not make the profits it hopes to make in that location, it just packs up and leaves a cavity in the community. Wal-Mart, in no uncertain terms, is a corporate pimp that uses people and uses communities to bolster its bottom line. It is a mobile economic plantation seeking to further enslave communities and people. And if we don't stand up, our people will continue to suffer. If we don't stand up, our communities will be ravished. What would it look like for churches to stand together as a community in various cities? What would it look like for coalitions locally and nationally to stand up to this giant and slay it with the stones of righteousness? Until Wal-Mart pays its workers a fair living wage, until Wal-Mart allows its workers to unionize, until Wal-Mart provides affordable health care, and until Wal-Mart stops the discrimination, we have decided at Trinity United Church of Christ to boycott Wal-Mart.

On a Sunday morning—right after we welcomed the visitors and right before the pastor's concerns—we passed out letters that were signed by members of the congregation. The letter detailed Wal-Mart's practices and urged the company to change them. About two weeks after we sent over 6,500 letters to Bensenville, Arkansas, Wal-Mart's corporate headquarters, we got a call from the executive vice president saying he wanted to meet with us.

I pray that these paradigms have shed a little light on how we may make justice a priority in our respective parishes. The paradigm for justice ministries in the church must serve the parishioner in need as well as fight for proper policies in the respective area of concern. The paradigm for church collaborative ministries urges us to walk together as congregations under Christ to fight for justice in our varied and collective contexts.

And these are not the only paradigms in terms of doing justice ministries. You may not use these paradigms, but I urge you to do something. Saint Sabina's congregation in Chicago was able to close all liquor stores around their church as well as all corner stores that sold drug paraphernalia. But here's the praise report: not only did they close them down, but they also bought the properties and opened a church-owned store that now provides jobs for the same ones who may have been victims of that drug paraphernalia.

In this sending forth moment, I am reminded of the words of Mark 6:7, when the Lord sent out his disciples and gave them authority over unclean spirits. These disciples were on a mission from the master. He sent them out as partners, two by two. He knew that partnership was essential to getting the work done. We cannot do this thing alone; we've got to work together. He told them to pack light. Don't be concerned with the bling bling. That's not what this mission is about. He told them to persevere, to keep on keeping on. Even when a house won't welcome you, shake that dust off, and keep stepping. Doing justice isn't going to be popular all the time, but we've got to persevere. For the Lord didn't call us to be popular; the Lord called us to be faithful. Doing justice may not get you invited to some of those press conferences and breakfasts you like to go to, but we've got to persevere. The Lord told his disciples to partner, to pack light, to persevere, and the disciples then proceeded with the power of God in them. They cast out many demons and cured the sick. As we are sent forth, there are all kinds of demons and sick people and institutions in our communities. But thanks be to God, God has given us that same Spirit that brings good news to the poor, opens blinded eyes, and proclaims release to those who are captives.

So as we leave this mountaintop experience to return to the valleys in which we work, let us go in the words of Dr. Renita Weems, "standing on the shoulders of our ancestors": Samuel DeWitt Proctor, Miles Jerome Jones, Jarena Lee, and Harriet Tubman. But ultimately, let us look to that great ancestor who came in the cause of freedom and liberation, Jesus, the revolutionary leader. Let us leave on our mission from the master, loading the wagons with the strength of our ancestors, imbued by the power of the spirit to turn this world upside down. Don't just speak about it; be about it. In the words of our anthem, "shadowed beneath thy hand, may we forever stand, true to our God, true to our native land!"

20.

The Black Church in the Age of False Prophets

An Interview with Gayraud Wilmore

Iva Carruthers (IC):   How do you account for the seemingly diminished and marginalized prophetic and liberating voice of the Black church over the past thirty years?

Gayraud Wilmore (GW):   That would take us back to 1974, Dr. Carruthers, and that is a long time in a life's span. A lot of water has flowed over the dam since the early seventies. In fact, the dam that some of us tried to build against the flood of white retrenchment and Black conservatism that followed the 1960s had all but caved in by the end of the twentieth century.

By this time, many of the great Black prophets of that century who influenced our churches—Marcus Garvey, William M. Trotter, W. E. B. DuBois, Ida B. Wells, Reverdy Ransom, Adam Clayton Powell Jr., A. Phillip Randolph, Nannie Helen Burroughs, Fannie Lou Hamer, and of course Martin and Malcolm—are all gone to their reward, but they are no longer held in high esteem by the middle-aged, middle-class church leaders of today. The watchword of today's mega-church evangelists, old-style bureaucrats and bishops, Bible teachers and preachers is: "Be cool. Keep your nose out of radical and controversial questions; stay out of trouble. If the people in the pews don't demand it, don't you command it!"

Of course, in popular culture the pendulum swings back to the opposite side of the clock. Today the voice of the Black church is all but a deafening silence. The burning issues of the twenty-first century—preventive war, terrorism, gay rights, human sexuality, family structures and values, the hip-hop culture, prison construction and reform, abortion, stem-cell research, genocide and ethnic cleansing,

Afrocentrism and the explosion of African Christianity, globalism, HIV/AIDS and the desperate needs of the Two-Thirds World—are scarcely touched by our Sunday sermons, conference addresses, church governing bodies, or literature.

I would pick 1968 as the beginning of Black Christian "know-nothingism," and the consequence has been a church in anti-biblical criticism, anti-intellectual, and anti-social action captivity.

IC: What new or old forms of theological reflection and doing ministry or church organization do you think are required to put the Black church on a corrective course?

GW: I think the times demand new approaches to basic theological issues—first the nature and authority of the Bible; then God, Jesus Christ, Holy Spirit, and the church; then humankind, both created and artificial nature, and eschatology. I said new, not novel. Our faithful reflection, ministry, and ecclesiology ought to be grounded in basic Reformation creeds and confessions, which I believe reflect—however imperfectly—the essence of a fairly common apostolic faith in the first five centuries. I cannot discount, as apparently many preachers can, the two thousand years of church history. But creedal statements—and we all honor them in one form or another—should be perennially reformed according to the change of times and seasons without losing the fundamental message of Jesus' life and teachings. This is the time of inescapable global shrinkage and intensified international and inter-group relations, and, as far as African Americans are concerned, it is a season of the devolution of ethnic identity and communal cement in an attempt to escape into personal anonymity and "rugged individualism." That may be fine for the middle class, but we still have a lot of poor folk who need a community to stand together and to fight. And as long as American racism persists, the Black middle class had better regroup its own forces. As the enemy's position changes and old strategies become ineffective, we have to change and adopt new strategies and tactics, always building anew upon what the past has taught us.

I use the word "fight" a lot because I believe that the apostle Paul is right when he says that we continually struggle, we resist, we wrestle against "principalities and powers" (Eph. 6:12). That is the nature and destiny of human life, and so much more so for Christians.

Black theology, as developed by scholars like Cone, Roberts, Grant, and Brown Douglas, is a theology of struggle, and we have by no means exhausted its resources. The ministries and church organizations developed by Gardner Taylor, Vinton Anderson, James Forbes, Mark Lomax, Dennis Wiley, Cynthia Hale, Calvin Butts,

Otis Moss Jr., Yvonne Delk, and Jeremiah Wright (and younger people, both lay and clergy, about whom I have heard but have not observed) are keyed to the changing times and seasons. They have not stopped listening and reading and growing and experimenting. They continue to explore the core and periphery of Black theology and the lessons we learned in the twentieth century: to fight and never turn back, to do theology as well as talk about it, to always do the research, to teach your people to read the newspapers as well as the Bible, to deploy the church in all the structures of the secular community, to always be engaged in struggle for Africa, to be glad to work with whites who have had that "second conversion," and to wage war against the demonic powers of this age without becoming hypocritical, bitter, or disillusioned.

IC: As you envision the Black church of the future, what do you see as the unique role or contribution of womanist theology and women in ministry?

GW: That's a question that I tried politely to evade until my last book. Not men but women should tell us what women envision for the future in terms of their contribution and role. I always say to the sisters that they must fight to establish their own place, to stand on it, and to make their own contributions—not to expect anyone to make them a gift. Black people fought side by side in the late 1960s to establish and credentialize Black theology in the church and the academy. Nobody gave us space or status. Black professors and their students had to fight for it in the church, the seminary, the university, and the publishing world. Womanist scholars have done the same thing and must continue to do it, with or without the approbation and support of men.

Womanist theology needs more exposure everywhere. It needs to be talked about, written about, studied, and explained as a legitimate way of doing theology by and for African American women, who are not hostile to or in competition with Black theology in general, but in a necessary way complementing, challenging, and completing the Black perspective on Christian faith. It needs to present itself, as I think women like Delores Williams, Iva Carruthers, and Linda Thomas have done, as the natural custodian of Black culture, which is itself the vibrant, generative environment through which theology and spirituality express and authenticate themselves. And it is precisely over this cultural matrix that Black women, as bearers and educators of our children and as preservers of "Black family values," have exercised dominion in the past and must do so into the foreseeable future.

Women will, I think, soon overtake the number of men going into the ministry and earning terminal degrees in the theological disciplines. What this will mean for the Black church no one knows. But it seems realistic that unless women organize themselves to fight for and take charge of our theological, spiritual, and ecclesiastical necessities, they will inevitably subsume their special vision of the direction of Black culture and religion under the magisterial precedence that was long ago established by men. Not that men have become irrelevant to the future of theology, but our women need no longer walk behind us or assume minority status in the preservation, definition, and extension of the affairs of church and culture. I tried to say that in *Pragmatic Spirituality*, but the women need to say it for themselves. And they need to say and demonstrate it side by side with their poor and powerless sisters in society and in the church. It will be an error of enormous consequence if Black women scholars and intellectuals ignore or bypass their sisters who already dominate the Black church numerically but continue to permit men to lead them by virtue of some mistaken idea of natural right.

That's as much as I dare say about the role and function of women in the Black church and the academy. It's already gotten me in enough trouble with too many brothers who simply do not understand!

IC: The Black church is clearly not monolithic. Is the diversity of the Black church today substantially different in kind, substance, and/or significance from the diversity of the past?

GW: Yes, I think so. In my day we were either Baptist, Methodist, or Pentecostal. Older men ran the churches and fraternal organizations. The women and children were in auxiliaries. Our kids were in Sunday school and in the back pews of the sanctuary until their adolescence. We were all essentially orthodox in our theology—generally following white neoorthodox or "evangelical" theologians and conservative Christian educators. Our congregations were more mixed than they are today in the sense that the poor, the middle class, and the wealthy sat side by side in the pews, but congregations were more homogeneous as far as the beliefs and values by which people lived are concerned. Then many more of us were poor and not well educated, and we felt both oppressed without and repressed within—we "minded our manners."

Today, looking down from the pulpit on a Sunday morning, you don't know what you have out there. Clearly, not many are poor and oppressed in the ordinary sense. The young people are gone. You really don't know what people believe, if they believe anything. Take a pop quiz to find out the biblical and theological knowledge of any Sunday congregation, and most of us would be shocked to discover the ignorance of people we've been preaching to for twenty or thirty years. Many of them don't reveal what they actually believe. Among the congregation we can find agnostics, practical atheists, younger members on the verge of going over to Islam, yoga practitioners and some curious about other Eastern religions, adherents of various TV and radio evangelists, younger people who are attracted only to gospel music and the entertainment of Sunday performances, people exploring radical Black theology, and folks who are proverbially at sea—drifting to and fro among a variety of operative worldviews, cults, and Christian bookstore theologians.

The significance of this situation is for me the challenge to find a common denominator among this diverse group of nominal Christians and make it the basis of reconstruction, unity, and mission. With important qualifications noted, what we have in common on Sunday morning is our skin color (and some us are "dark white"); we have our identity and sensibility of being African American—a Black minority of about 12 percent in a nation of people who are still predominantly white, middle-class, and politically, economically, and socially conservative.

I believe that this gives us an opportunity to emphasize that without losing a certain amount of healthy variety, we can develop our unity and utility for God's realm as Afrocentric Christians who are on a mission of love and justice, of human equality, rehabilitation, and cultural and religious reconstruction for the enhancement of human life and to the glory of God through our Lord Jesus Christ. That is for me "the fruit" spoken of by the writer of the Letter to the Colossians (1:6), the pragmatic meaning of salvation, and the implication of almost everything that is said about the meaning of the Christian faith in that first chapter of Colossians.

IC: The growth and epicenter of the Christian tradition have certainly moved away from the West toward Africa and Asia. What new opportunities, challenges, or barriers does this movement have for the mission of the Black church?

GW: Frankly, I am astonished at how ignorant African American Christians seem to be of what is happening in Africa today—and when you add Asia, the explosion of Christianity in the Southern Hemisphere blows me out of my rocking chair! According to their alacrity in finally bringing some native Africans into the episcopacy at the last quadrennial, the AME Church seems to have woken up, but the rest of us lag behind. As far as Africa is concerned, it holds the future of Christianity in its hand. Almost ten years ago Elizabeth Isichei reminded us that some statistics being bandied about in the 1990s had a credibility no sensible follower of Jesus Christ could ignore. She wrote, "There were 10 million African Christians in 1900, 143 million in 1970, and there will be 393 million in the year 2000, which would mean that 1 in 5 of all Christians would be African."[1] Moreover, as we now know, the overwhelming majority of these African Christians—1,055 million or 44 percent of world Christianity—will belong to African Initiated and Pentecostal churches.[2]

Why are we African American Christians not more excited about this? Why do our leaders not see the significance of our role, before the middle of the twenty-first century, as older and somewhat more experienced, if spoiled, Christians—as we encounter our brother and sister followers of Jesus Christ across the Atlantic? What, for example, does Black theology in the United States have to say to these brothers and sisters, if anything?

These are what I take to be the raw implications of your question, Dr. Carruthers, and I tremble to even speculate about them. I certainly cannot give any final answers. One fact smashes my brain like a sledgehammer, and that is: this African church—whether independent or born of European and American missions—is considerably more conservative than the Black churches of this country, and they will undoubtedly challenge what we have, perhaps without warrant, considered our precedence as the exponent of an Afrocentric Christian faith by virtue of our experience as a slave church, our understanding of the theology of struggle against a demonic racism, and our more recent experience as a justice-seeking church under the leadership of Martin Luther King Jr.

I believe that we have something to give, in that regard, as well as much to learn from the Pentecostal spirituality of the African Initiated Churches (AICs), but are we ready for such a challenge? I doubt it. We are much too fractured, much too unsure about what we believe, much too fuzzy about what should heal our vaunted denominationalism, much too dependent upon white theology—to be quite frank about it—to sit across the table from our African sisters and brothers and expound a perspective on the Christian faith and mission that will help them to see that biblical religion has to do with more than unsullied holiness, an uncritical belief in biblical inerrancy, emotionalism in worship, heterosexual absolutism, patriarchal domination, and apolitical neutrality in the face of monstrous wrongs in the world today. Until we face up to and deal with these issues on this side of the Atlantic, we African American Christians will be devastated when we meet in theological dialogue with mission partners in Africa and Asia.

On the other hand, there are many good opportunities for us to come together in mutually beneficial ways if we are alert to some and are willing to create others. I'm thinking now of the work that my dear departed brother Bongani A. Mazibuko was doing in South Africa before his untimely death. He was developing a new pedagogy for the churches and universities that would bring together the schooled and unschooled clergy and laity to learn a liberating curriculum of research and action from each other. That work is described in a remarkable Festschrift in honor of Mazibuko, entitled *Mission Is Crossing Frontiers*.[3] This collection of essays is edited by Roswith Gerloff, who herself is one of the most knowledgeable missiologists in Europe and Africa on the question you are raising with me. Her book is not well known in the United States, and I urge everyone interested in the changing face of Christianity in Africa and among Africans living in Europe to order and read it.

One of the "new opportunities" for both African and African American church leaders and educators is the possibility of developing projects like the one developed by Bongani Mazibuko, when he was dean of the faculty of theology at the University of Durban-Westville, with Jack Johnson-Hill, a professor of ethics and missiology at the same university. In the Gerloff book you will find an excellent case study of the "Umlazi Project" in nonformal theological education. It clearly delineates the new methodology Mazibuko introduced for facilitating liberative learning and action among "non-credentialed" pastors and laypeople in South Africa. It should not take an unusual amount of imagination to see how what is being done in the Durban-Westville context can be replicated in metropolitan centers and rural areas in the United States and the Caribbean. In the 1980s Bongani studied what Louis-Charles Harvey and I were trying to do with our "Alternate Education Program" at Colgate Rochester, and, taking the germ idea to Birmingham, England, and South Africa, he improved upon it and demonstrated the real possibility of liberative theological education at the grass roots that could transform the Black church on both sides of the Atlantic.

Second, I cannot over-emphasize the tremendous opportunity we African American Christians have to relate to counterparts in Africa by making the HIV/AIDS pandemic there one of our top-level priorities of our denominations and local congregations. Individual mission committees can participate in the Home-Based Care Kit Program, which involves supplying, packing, and shipping to African churches boxes containing essential items for the care of ten AIDS patients— bath towels, rubber gloves, calamine lotion, sterile gauze, plastic sheets and aprons, and so forth—which local people are trained to use with persons suffering from AIDS. Each kit costs from $100 to $200 in the United States and is accompanied by at least $100 for the training of volunteers in the participating African country, who organize, distribute, and are taught to use the kits for local persons stricken with the disease. Some U.S. churches and the African American caucus of the Presbyterian Church, U.S.A., have been sending kits to Malawi and Kenya since 2003. I would urge our denominations and congregations to get in touch with the people who are promoting this outreach to Africa and join in the AIDS Home-Based Care Kit Program. Of course, we must put more pressure on our government and the multinational corporations to get to the preventative heart of the HIV/AIDS problem in the United States and all over the world, but this project of mercy and love in behalf of individual sufferers is an immediate way for congregations to be involved. Everyone seems to be quoting the shocking statistics, but too few of us are doing what we can to meet the daily needs of the thousands of individuals who are sick and dying. Everyone wants to be more spiritual, but this is another example of what I call pragmatic spirituality.

Finally, I believe we need to do much more in preparing African American church members to understand the significance of what is going on in Africa today in terms of the explosion of the Christian gospel. This will require better literature on the African mission and African Initiated Churches, a broad revision of our church school materials and teacher training, more sermons that target Africa, missiology, and ecumenical efforts to dialogue and partner with Africans already in the United States (many of whom are presently worshiping in their own churches in our midst without any sense that African American Christians desire or are ready to dialogue with them). Connections and friendship with an increasing number of African Christian immigrants to this country should be the first step in learning about the conditions on the continent and making contact with congregations in Africa that are anxious and able to be mission partners with us.

IC: As one who was such an active participant and witness to the emergence of Black liberation theology, what has been your biggest disappointment about the planting of liberation theology or lack thereof in the life of the Black church?

GW: I think my greatest disappointment is the failure of our most significant and resourceful ecumenical agency—the Congress of National Black Churches (CNBC)—to embrace the insights and affirmations of Black liberation theology, stamp them with its imprimatur, and convey them to the thousands of local congregations, pastors, evangelists, and church school teachers who represent the official cadres of the CNBC's participating denominations. A part of my chagrin about that failure has been the disinclination of the CNBC to give assent to the fact that the term "Black church" includes the more than three million African Americans who worship in Black congregations that are a part of predominantly white denominations. That barrier has prevented many of us from participating in the ecumenical mainstream of African American churches and, thereby, denied that movement of the considerable experience, wisdom, and material resources of congregants, pastors, and teachers who have remained in the white churches, not as flunkies but as goads, mentors, and witnesses to both the sin of American racism and the spiritual unity of the Body of Christ. The largest number of people excluded from the conclaves of the seven or eight largest Black denominations are the Black Roman Catholics. Numbering over two million in 2000, they are no less the recipients of our great heritage than are Baptists, Methodists, and Pentecostals. To deny ourselves of what Pope Paul VI called the "gift of [their] Blackness" when he addressed African Catholics is a grievous error and to our everlasting shame.

I don't want to be misunderstood here. I do not blame any particular person or group of persons for this lamentable situation. It is the consequence of history, the political inertia that grips most religious institutions. But we can do something about it. In the past decade two or three attempts were made without success. I am hoping that your new organization, the Samuel DeWitt Proctor Conference, Inc., will be able to rectify this exclusivity on the part of our current interchurch movement and bring us all together in life and work as we were when the first AME bishop, Richard Allen, in the early nineteenth century headed a progressive group of African American pastors and laypeople in the city of Philadelphia without regard for denomination.

But I must briefly mention other disappointments before we close. On other occasions I have talked about seminary graduates whose preaching and public ministries give no hint that they ever earned a Master of Divinity degree after spending seven years in college and graduate school. That probably has something to do with those who teach as well as those who learned from them. I plead guilty. Black liberation theologians and other seminary professors have simply not instructed well enough about how to help ordinary folks in the pews become the vanguard of a new interpretation of that old, old story of Jesus and his love. Nor have our Black seminaries helped. We have not yet been able to come together as educational institutions to define what we mean by African American theological education at all levels of the church's life and how it differs from what is taught in most predominantly white seminaries and universities that have no viable Black Church Studies program. I weep for the men and women I have taught who are out there struggling but who have little to show for what they presumably learned from me and scholars of my generation. There are, I hasten to say, some prominent exceptions whose names I could call, but they are an unheralded minority in today's climate of charismatic showmanship, biblical literalism, and historical and cultural "know-nothingism."

We desperately need to do an audit of the Black church and its educational institutions and publishing houses. Where are we now? What do we propose to preach and teach? Our denominations need to rid themselves of institutional narcissism and cut back on organizational housekeeping so that the people can concentrate on mission in their own communities and the Two-Thirds World. Those of us in the so-called mainline churches need to rid ourselves of low self-esteem and an inferiority complex vis-à-vis the mega-church phenomenon. Words such as liberation, social justice, God-talk, Black culture, biblical criticism, Afrocentrism, human sexuality, gender equality, interfaith, interracial, and worldwide ecumenism are still germane to the comprehensive cultural vocation of the African American church, if we will but give them evocative content and demonstration in the home, the schools, and the public square.

The Black church, if we can speak that way of this incredibly complex and diverse institution we belong to, needs to come out of many closets and face the realities and challenges of the twenty-first century. We will be able to do that for the redemption of humankind and the glory of God when we stop fussing over homosexuality and denominationalism, stop displaying our righteous indignation against the world God has left us whether we like it or not, stop preening and posturing, and come together to take our place with the historic Christian families of the postmodern world in the great drama of liberation and reconciliation to which we have been called and consigned.

Notes

Chapter 2—The Sheep and the Goats

1. Earl Paulk quoted in the *Atlanta Constitution*, March 3, 1987, A4, as cited by Gayraud S. Wilmore, "Black Theology at the Turn of the Century: Some Unmet Needs and Challenges," in Dwight N. Hopkins, ed., *Black Faith and Public Talk: Critical Essays on James H. Cone's Black Theology and Black Power* (Maryknoll, NY: Orbis, 1999), 243.

2. Nelson Mandela, "Renewal and Renaissance: Towards a New World Order," lecture given at the Oxford Centre for Islamic Studies, Oxford, England, July 11, 1997; available at www.anc.org.za/ancdocs/history/mandela/1997/sp970711c.html.

3. Linda E. Thomas, *Under the Canopy: Ritual Process and Spiritual Resilience in South Africa* (Columbia: University of South Carolina Press, 1999), 7.

4. Martin Luther King Jr., Christmas Sermon, Ebenezer Baptist Church, Atlanta, Georgia, December 24, 1967.

Chapter 3—From Vision to Action

1. Zan Wesley Holmes Jr., *Encountering Jesus* (Nashville: Abingdon, 1992).

2. Mary McLeod Bethune, "Faith That Moved a Dump Heap," *Who* (June 1941).

3. Martin Luther King Jr., "Letter from a Birmingham Jail," in *Why We Can't Wait* (New York: Signet, 1964).

Chapter 4—Piety and Liberation

1. See "The Life and Religious Experience of Jarena Lee," in William L. Andrews, ed., *Sisters of the Spirit: Three Black Women's Autobiographies of the Nineteenth Century*, Religion in North America (Bloomington: Indiana University Press, 1986), 25–48.

2. See "A 'Disquieting' Negro Petition to Congress, 1800," in Herbert Aptheker, ed., *A Documentary History of the Negro People in the United States*, vol. 1 (New York: Citadel, 1968), 44.

3. See "A Secret Organization For Freedom," in Aptheker, *Documentary History*, 378–80.

4. In "Greetings of Olivet Baptist Church, Celebrating the Seventy-Second Anniversary of the Church and Six Years Pastorate of Dr. L. K. Williams, 1922" (n.p., 1922), 11.

5. One might inquire, however, as to whether those groups asserting an alternative identity were doing so at the cost of assenting to what whites had claimed, namely, that being Black was a degraded, undesirable state.

6. Cited in Aptheker, *Documentary History*, 232.

7. Congress of National Black Churches newsletter, *Visions* 8/1 (winter 1998/spring 1999).

8. C. Eric Lincoln and Lawrence Mamiya, *The Black Church in the African American Experience* (Durham, NC: Duke University Press, 1990).

9. The Marx article is reprinted in August Meier and Elliott T. Rudwick, eds., *The Making of Black America*, vol. 2 (New York: Atheneum, 1971), 62–75.

10. Lincoln and Mamiya, *The Black Church*, 399.

11. Ibid., 400–404.

12. James Henry Harris, "Practicing Liberation in the Black Church," www.religion-online.org/showarticle.asp?title=778.

13. Ibid.

14. W. Franklyn Richardson, "The Black Church's Twenty-First Century Challenge," *Essence* (August 1999).

Chapter 6—Liberating the Ancient Utterances of African People

1. George Wells Parker, "The Children of the Sun" (pamphlet published by Hamitic League of the World, 1918).

2. Ayi Kwei Armah, *Two Thousand Seasons* (London: Heinemann, 1979).

3. Brooke Medicine Eagle, "Foreword," in Sobonfu Somé, *Welcoming Spirit Home: Ancient African Teachings to Celebrate Children and Community* (Novato, CA: New World Library, 1999), ix.

4. Sobonfu Somé, *Welcoming Spirit Home*.

5. *The Book of the Dead: The Papyrus of Ani in the British Museum*, trans. E. A. Wallis Budge (New York: Dover, 1967), xcii–xciii.

6. Daniel Defoe, *The Life and Strange Surprising Adventures of Robinson Crusoe* (London: W. Taylor, 1719), chap. 6.

7. Martin Luther King Jr., speech delivered to Clergy and Laity Concerned, Riverside Church, New York City, April 4, 1967; text available at www.hartford-hwp.com/archives/45a/058.html.

8. Zbigniew Brzezinski, *The Grand Chessboard: American Primacy and Its Geostrategic Imperatives* (New York: Basic, 1998), 21.

9. Ibid., 31.

Chapter 7—The Prophetic Imperative

1. Obery M. Hendricks Jr., "I Am the Holy Dope Dealer: The Problem with Gospel Music Today," in James Abbington, ed., *Readings in African American Church Music and Worship* (Chicago: GIA, 2001), 553–90.

Chapter 8—Freeing the Captives

1. Michael Cunningham and Craig Marberry, *Crowns: Portraits of Black Women in Church Hats* (New York: Doubleday, 2000).

2. Tertullian, *On the Apparel of Women* 1.1.4–7.

3. Augustine, *Letters*, 243:10.

4. J. Lee Grady, *Ten Lies the Church Tells Women: How the Bible Has Been Misused to Keep Women in Spiritual Bondage* (Lake Mary, FL: Creation House, 2000).

5. For a critical review of *Ten Lies* by an evangelical feminist scholar, see Nancy A. Hardesty's review in *EEWC Update* 26/1 (spring 2002); available at http://www.eewc.com/Reviews/Spring2002Lies.htm.

6. James M. Alsdurf, "Wife Abuse and the Church: The Response of Pastors," *Response to the Victimization of Women and Children* 8/1 (1985): 9–11.

7. A. Elaine Crawford, "From Victim to Vessel: Prolegomena to a Womanist Theology of Hope," PhD diss., Union Theological Seminary and Presbyterian School of Christian Education, Charlotte, North Carolina, 1999.

Chapter 9—The Biblical Basis for a Political Theology of Liberation

1. Randall C. Bailey, "The Danger of Ignoring One's Own Cultural Bias in Interpreting the Text," in R. S. Sugirtharajah, ed., *The Postcolonial Bible*, The Bible and Postcolonialism 1 (Sheffield: Sheffield Academic Press, 1998), 66–90.

2. Brian K. Blount, *Go Preach! Mark's Kingdom Message and the Black Church Today* (Maryknoll, NY: Orbis, 1998).

Chapter 10—And the Bible Says

1. Shawn Kelley, *Racializing Jesus: Race, Ideology, and the Formation of Modern Biblical Scholarship*, Biblical Limits (London: Routledge, 2002).

Chapter 11—The Priestly Faithful and Prophetically Courageous

1. Updated information from official reports of the Office of Economic Cooperation and Development is available at: www.globalissues.org/TradeRelated/Debt/USAid.asp?p=1#ForeignAidNumbersinChartsandGraphs As of 2003, the aid figures by country in terms of percentage of GNP were: Germany, 0.28; Japan, 0.2; United Kingdom, 0.34; and the United States, 0.14.

2. See Peter Singer, *Practical Ethics*, 2nd ed, (Cambridge: Cambridge University Press, 1993), 218–246.

3. Peter J. Gomes, *Life Before Death and Other Sermons* (Cambridge: Harvard University, in-house edition), 5:235–242.

Chapter 13—Keep the Pressure On

1. See William Douglas, "A Case of Race? One POW Acclaimed, Another Ignored," *Seattle Times*, November 9, 2003.

2. See "State of Texas to Overturn 39 Drug Convictions in Tulia: In 1999 One White Detective Arrested 15 Percent of the Town's African-American Population in Drug Sweep," *Democracy Now!* April 2, 2003; available at: www.democracynow.org/article.pl?sid=03/04/16/2156239.

Chapter 16—Born to Be a Witness

1. Langston Hughes, "Dreams," in *Collected Poems of Langston Hughes* (New York: Knopf, 1994).

Chapter 18—Black Church Leadership in the Age of AIDS

1. Kelly Brown Douglas, *Sexuality in the Black Church: A Womanist Perspective* (Maryknoll, NY: Orbis, 1999).

2. Dietrich Bonhoeffer, "After Ten Years," in *Letters and Papers from Prison*, enl. ed., ed. Eberhard Bethge (New York: Macmillan, 1971), 17.

3. Robert M. Franklin, *Another Day's Journey: Black Churches Confronting the American Crisis* (Minneapolis: Fortress Press, 1997).

4. Howard Thurman, *The Inward Journey* (New York: Harper, 1961).

Chapter 19—At the Table

1. Renita J. Weems, *Listening for God: A Minister's Journey through Silence and Doubt* (New York: Simon & Schuster, 1999), 7.

Chapter 20—The Black Church in the Age of False Prophets

1. Elizabeth Isichei, *The History of Christianity in Africa: From Antiquity to the Present* (Grand Rapids: Eerdmans; Lawrenceville, NJ: Africa World, 1995), 1.

2. These statistics are estimated by David R. Barrett in *World Christian Encyclopaedia*, updated in *International Bulletin of Missionary Research*.

3. Roswith Gerloff, ed., *Mission Is Crossing Frontiers: Essays in Honor of the Late Bongani A. Mazibuko, 1932–1997* (Pietermaritzburg, South Africa: Cluster, 2003).